WHEN MIND STOPS, THE MAGIC BEGINS

WHEN MIND STOPS, THE MAGIC BEGINS

HOW TO *LIVE FREELY* & DO WHAT NEEDS TO BE DONE

Authored by

KAMAL KHURANA

penmanbooks.com

Penman Books

Office No. 303, Kumar House Building,
D Block, Central Market, Opp PVR Cinema,
Prashant Vihar, Delhi 110085, India
Website: www.penmanbooks.com
Email: publish@penmanbooks.com

First Published by Penman Books 2019

Title: When Mind Stops, The Magic Begins
ISBN: 978-93-89024-32-6

An Attempt to Demystify Spirituality
to Provide Practical Solutions for
Everyday Life Problems

~~~
~~~

If you want to live happily,
only by being in the *no mind* state,
you can discover your true self,
your true nature, and real happiness.

—Kamal Khurana

Introduction

Thoughts Behind This Book

It took me close to three decades to learn how to end all my suffering, and here I am today, COMPLETELY FEARLESS.

My learning helped me live a life of freedom, and thereby, now, I have a choice to LIVE. I don't live in the future, so I don't die every moment. I won my mind, and now, my mind works the way it must.

On discovering this unique way to conquer the mind, I felt the need to share it with everyone. I call it *Inner Self Integration*.

Trust me, when you finish this book, and when you genuinely apply the simple techniques that comprise a few parts of *Inner Self Integration*, like thousands of my friends, you too will feel the need to learn the full technique. But it was not that easy for me to discover the true way of living.

Here's how it all happened…

Born into a simple middle-class family in New Delhi, I could never think about big concepts like 'the purpose of existence.' Like all other teenagers, I used to watch music channels on television (TV) and listen to pop songs. I had my own dream world where I was a hero.

I used to think I was nothing, and I wanted to be something. In a way, it was a pursuit to be something or someone. But the rubber used to hit the road every Valentine's Day, leaving me in despair. School was a nightmare as well, as I couldn't understand much in class, and feared the days when the exams would be held. The real world made me feel very low about myself.

Thankfully, somehow I managed to pass the final exams at the end of school term. Like most mediocre kids, I found respite in my dream world. I used to aspire big but ended up with a deep sense of failure every time.

This further deepened my belief that I was nothing, and I became even more desperate wanted to become 'something.'

Finally, I succeeded in securing admission to a management course and learnt that one needs to think out of the box to create a world of one's own. During my programme there, I met people from diverse backgrounds—the middle-class to the most elite, the not so intelligent to intellectuals. This changed something in my thought process.

With all the zeal in my heart, I joined my father's telecom business. I assumed that I could win customers and rule the markets with my postgraduate degree in marketing. I had learnt to sell anything. I still thought that I was a nobody, but the difference was, I realised I could be a *somebody*.

My dad had started with a penny in his pocket and earned his fortune in the private telecom industry. And when my turn came, in his mind, he had retired. When I joined his business, what I never expected happened. He couldn't comprehend my vision for his business. When I look back at it now, it all sounds funny; but back then, it wasn't. I tried my luck and attempted to pave my way to fortune, but somewhere at the end of the fourth year of being in his business, I realised that I was on the wrong train. By then, I was twenty-seven.

I observed my other batch mates employed in corporate jobs and doing well for themselves. I felt they had achieved something, whereas I was still a nobody. Little did I know, destiny had an amazing plan for me.

Suddenly, a weird business idea sprouted in my mind. I wanted to be a practicing psychologist—a relationship expert, to be specific. The thought behind it was that if I was good at selling, I could sell conceptual ideas to help the mind work constructively. I could help people sort out their lives. Thereon, I started my studies in psychology.

As I didn't belong to the field, I had to prove my mettle. With that in mind, I studied hundreds of books and took dozens of courses, a few from outside of India as well. I was lucky as I had some of the best teachers in the field.

I then started my small-time practice. For the first time in life, I was very excited for two reasons. One, it was my own baby, and two, with the passage of time, I became good at my work. I had the skill of helping people learn how to be happy and functional. By this time, I developed a hazy belief that I was a somebody or that I had finally become something.

The most interesting part of my journey was that the more I interacted with my clients, the more I discovered that there was something much deeper than the functioning of the conscious and subconscious mind. I sensed that the Science of psychology was still shallow and incomplete. It became evident to me that the misery of mankind was only because of the mind and the obsessive thinking that the mind engages in, round the clock.

Having heard hundreds of clients, my system felt burdened. I felt like I knew life way beyond my years. It seemed to me that I had lived the lives of all those hundreds of people. I sensed that somewhere amidst it all, I was trying to discover myself in every client. I was observing issues that centred righteousness and ownership in every client's story. Even though I successfully helped people with their issues, with every passing day, I was more and more affected by the global state of affairs.

I now realise that it was Nihilism that was killing me inside. Nihilism is a belief that all of life is meaningless. A belief, that I was not just what I was doing at the time, found strength within me. So after listening to the similar plight of thousands of people, I developed a profound inquisitiveness to learn the answers to questions such as *Why are things the way they are? Why does the universe exist? Why do I exist?* And finally, *Who am I*? It was the seed of a big tree that was yet to take birth.

These feelings eventually led to a change in my direction. I met teachers who introduced me to the deeper Science, **Spirituality**. They were always mentioning the subject, but I was not ready to comprehend their indications. The word *Spiritual* comes from the word *Spirit* which means "the vital principle or animating force behind all living beings—the breath."

For this, I had to briefly study all the sciences, all the basic concepts as described by the researches of scientists—ranging from the theory of relativity to the concepts of light, heat, the Big Bang theory, and evolution. And finally, I got a chance to briefly experience most schools of thought in the domains of spirituality and religion.

After learning the reasons behind the pain and suffering of people, I wanted to discover the ultimate way to be happy and peaceful. My inquisitiveness to study the world outside brought me to the inner journey, and I discovered my answer—"*I am*."

The answer matched the messages of the scriptures, religions, and the sciences. This book is a medium to share and explain that precious answer which is a quick way to arrive at innate, eternal peace.

It is strange that the minute you discover this precious way, you will feel like sharing it with your close ones (the ones you call your own) yourself. The same way, this book is an attempt to share it with you, as I realised that you too belong to me. I genuinely want you to get the simple and practical solution to all life problems—*The Self.*

I have been blessed from the moment I discovered "The Self" – "*I*." I live life fully every day, since then. Life is a play for me, and there is joy everywhere. Situations appear merely as situations and nothing more. I am in action every moment, as an obvious result of the breathing in my body, yet I am effortless in the motion of life. Life is like a momentum where I float in peace.

I assure you the same life, where you will accomplish all that you deserve. And all this will happen and will make a difference—there will be joy within and around you. All you need to do is to just follow what I learnt, and you will witness the magic of the truth, which will be empirically tested and proven to you. When I saw structure getting added to my work, a new foolproof technique was born and it was named *Inner Self Integration*.

Contents

PART *One*

Entrapment Called The Mind

All the situations are outside of you. By this, I mean that all of them are passive. It is how you feel that makes it different. Have you ever thought why it is pleasant for a child to see raindrops falling on his skin, whereas it is a matter of worry for you when the same drops fall on your expensive business suit? Have you ever wondered why you are so negatively affected? It is the thinking that happens in the mind that makes it all different for you.

Q: Are we not supposed to think if something happens and impacts us?

A: The answer is NO. It true that at present, you can't stop the thinking. And it is the thinking that is your disease. *Disease – Dis-Ease* means 'Not in Ease.' Constant thinking turns the mind into a madhouse. And the funny part is that despite thinking so much, you still remain where you are; rather, worse. And in this process of thinking, you waste a lot of time—your active life.

Q: Should nobody in the world think?

A: Nobody knows how to 'not think.' Surely, some people know how to distract the mind, but being out of the trap of the mind calls for some awareness. The world has misery because people think. Thinking is an attempt aimed at trying to change, which is what we call the reaction.

Reaction has the inertia of the action that has happened. The action in itself was neutral, but how it was perceived by the experiencer makes all the difference. And it is the way the incident or action was perceived. Perceiving and thinking lead the reaction.

If perceiving and thinking change, the world will change. Then, there will be an effortless response, irrespective of the incident. This response is the righteous response. Your world will change, thereby effecting change in your life (i.e., the way you live). In *Inner Self Integration*, you will learn about the term "righteous."

Q: Do we have a choice to live a happy, free life where we are not engaged in obsessive thinking?

A: First, know where the obsessive thinking is happening.

Where exactly do you think the constant noise and useless thoughts are running continuously?

The answer is '**The Mind.**'

This means that if the goal is a **Free, Happy, Accomplished Life**, the hurdle is in the mind, because even if you get all the things that you aspire towards today, your mind will set itself up to a new frustration to attain the next level of your desires, and the next, and then, the next.

Q: It is written in almost all the scriptures that to shut the mind, we need to stop aspiring. But if we stop aspiring, will our life not stop? How will we survive in this world then?

A: There is a need to understand the difference between effortless *natural progression of the world* and *aspiring*. Progression is certain and inevitable. Here, it is called the *Truth*. But aspiration indicates scarcity. Scarcity is pain.

This sense of scarcity is the act of the mind, and this is the trap. You are not supposed to stop living or stop the process of life. The difference is about voluntary suffering and experiencing joyful movement.

Q: Does that mean we can never be free from the trap of the mind?

A: Yes, you can never be free unless you see that you are in the trap. You can be free only if you know that you are in the trap. This is the misery of the masses in today's world, and people are unaware of this.

Q: This way, aren't we trapping our own selves? Aren't we our mind?

A: Certainly, it is the mind. You need to distinguish yourself and the mind. Despite the existence of the mind and its trap, there are moments when the mind doesn't exist. For example, while sleeping, the mind ceases to exist.

But then, can you say that during the time the body sleeps, you don't exist? No, you exist, and at that time, the mind doesn't.

It is the natural mechanism of the body to shut your mind for a few hours. So this means the mind and you can be dealt with differently. Understanding the existence of the mind while you are awake is a knack you will develop when you have completely read and understood the concepts mentioned in this book.

CHAPTER
One

The Mind's Pain Game

It is the belief systems of the mind that make you think in a set pattern. Your set beliefs and thinking lead you to **feel** in a set pattern, which results in the set behavioral **response** from your end to the situation. And all this leads to the set way life always appears before you. This is what I call the pain game of the mind —'the thinking.'

Therefore, it is not the situations that cause pain, but the thinking. You will find most people cribbing and sulking because of the situations they are surrounded by. However, the truth is that the thinking (that people are surrounded by) results in the occurrence of the situation.

Let us understand the mind more...

Broadly, the pain game of the mind can be classified into two categories – *I want* and *I don't want.*

I want...

In 1859, Charles Darwin, the famous scientist, published a book on the *Origin of Species,* which delved into the origin of man and his history. Since then, thousands of researches have been conducted, that suggested monkeys were the ancestors of humans.

If you observe any species of the monkey family, you can see how restless monkeys are. You will see that they have to do something or the other. The only difference between monkeys and humans is that humans can pretend to be disciplined. This is because right from the time we go to kindergarten, humans are taught to be disciplined and mannered.

But what about the mind? However you may try to hide your restlessness, the game continues in the mind. The mind wants something more, something better, and perhaps the most important fact is that it 'wants something.' It will be wise to conclude that the mind *wants*.

This misery has lasted mankind thousands of years. As the mind *wants*, you begin your pursuit to attain the objects of the want. Objects of want, here, refer to desired things or situations.

Buddha has illustrated this concept of '**want'** very well.

Firstly, the want itself generates a feeling of **stress and fear** and a **feeling of *less***.

Secondly, to satisfy the mind's game of the 'want', you act; and in case the action doesn't lead to the **desired result** or the object of the 'want', there is **frustration**.

Thirdly, if the object of 'want' is not exactly how it was desired in the mind, **the frustration persists**.

And fourthly, if the object of 'want' is exactly or nearly how it was desired, the **birth of a new want** within occurs within a very short span of time. This is because the fulfilment of the 'want' leads to the illusion that all wants can be fulfilled. So, the disease starts.

This means that all the pursuit itself leads to four other pursuits, which further lead to the same outcome—frustration.

So we should conclude the game of the mind.

Q: **Does it mean that you should stop wanting anything, stop going to work, stop going to the grocery store, and stop breathing?**

A: The answer needs to be derived. As mentioned earlier, you need to find out the distinction between the two situations—

1. Do you **need** to be going to the grocery store? or
2. Do you **want** to go to the grocery store?

Now, consider the difference between the following two statements as well—

1. Do you **need** to buy the new car? or
2. Do you **want** to buy the new car?

Think about it—'Do you need the grocery, and do you need the new car?' Want is "**desiring greatly and wishing for**."

Need is **"being under the necessity of."**

The word *'necessary'* is the differentiator.

Mind you, I am not yet declaring what needs to be done, but simply asking you to observe and notice the distinction. It is an attempt to provoke the mind to think in a new way. Please be prepared and know that your mind will resist a lot.

Let us go a bit deeper...

Think about the following two scenarios.

SCENARIO 1. Is the grocery going to come up anyway because there is a need in the kitchen or is the scarcity in your mind the reason for the the grocery coming up?

SCENARIO 2. Is the car going to come up anyway because there is a need for a car or is the car going to come up because of the scarcity in your mind?

Certainly, the scarcity is in your mind. In any case, the grocery will come up as an automatic outcome in the world. It will come through you though. But the feeling of scarcity (and thereby, pain) is a choice that you always had and will always have. The choice to suffer or not is always with you. You will learn how to exercise that choice in the following chapters.

Mind you, even now, I am not declaring what needs to be done, but simply asking you to observe and notice the distinction. It is another attempt to provoke your mind to think in a new way. You may either understand what has been alluded to or you may not. Understanding is an active task and not accomplished by mere passive reading.

I Don't Want...

Very interestingly, there is another pain game of the mind—'the don't want.' Buddha has referred to this aversion as *Dwesha*.

You will hear yourself saying "I don't want this" or "I don't want that" very often.

And not only in terms of the present, you even make a declaration with regard to the future by saying "I can never take this", "I will never let this happen", "I will never do this", and so on.

Your mind carries an aversion towards a lot of things, and this leads to suffering every time you encounter those specific situations, people, or things. This means that the remote control to your suffering is inside your mind. Just as your mind employs **scarcity** as a pain game, it also employs **aversion** as another pain game.

Now think about the following two scenarios—

SCENARIO 1. While driving, do you stop at the red signal **because there is a need to be careful** or is it **because of your mind's aversion to accidents**?

SCENARIO 2. When you start to work, you discover that you have a flat tyre. Ask yourself, *Are you feeling frustrated* ***because of the punctured tyre,*** or *Is the frustration* ***due to your mind's aversion to the flat tyre?***

Mind you, even now, I am not declaring what needs to be done. I am simply making another attempt to provoke your mind to think of the pain game 'I don't want' in a new way.

Certainly, the aversion is in your mind. I don't say that you can or should be happy to see a flat tyre. Nobody can be happy in such a situation, but you still have a choice—to suffer or not to. You will have this choice when you learn to distinguish between the incident and your choice.

You will learn the way soon, in the following chapters of this book.

Q: Does it mean we should not want anything? If the answer is 'yes', we will be doing nothing if we don't want anything in life, won't we?

A: Please note, I said you get pain only when you want it. Understand the difference between what you need and what you want. As explained earlier, *want* is about 'desiring greatly' and 'wishing for', while *need* is about 'being in necessity of.' So necessity defines the cause of this world.

All that is necessary will keep happening on its own in this world. But the minute you think you want to change something, it leads to frustration. So, to *not want*, you simply fulfill the needs that need to be fulfilled, as per life's needs and not per your mind's needs.

This calls for creating a distinction between the mind and you. When you allow life to move the way it is moving, you don't get too trapped in the pain game of the mind.

Q: Can the mind ever be trained to stop this game of inflicting pain?

A: Yes, of course, it is possible. You will witness this happening to you. You will learn to bring your mind peace at good intervals, to begin with. After that, it depends on your practice. The practice is just about remembering the technique. You have to comfortably observe, understand, and finally tune your mind.

Q: Can we live in peace our entire lives?

A: Living in peace is a way of life. Knowing the characteristic of the mind is more important here. It is well said that whatever you measure gets controlled. The same way, when you observe your mind, you are out of the game the mind plays.

The mind will keep playing its game as long as the body lives, the only difference is that over time, with practice, you will relish the prodigy of this baby—the mind.

The baby will continue throwing its tantrums and take you on rides. You will be able to see those rides as joyrides. The peaceful moments will assume a larger a part of your life, and there will be very few dips.

CHAPTER *Two*

The Mind's Obsessive Thinking

In the books of psychology, **obsession** is defined as a continual thought, concept, picture, or urge that is experienced as invasive and not proper and results in significant fear, distress, and discomfort.

Do you engage in obsessive thinking several times in the day? The answer is 'yes' for most people. Some are aware of it, while some are not.

The mind is a system that works on its own. It receives inputs from the five senses—the eyes, ears, nose, skin, and the tongue. These senses create sensations that are perceived by the mind.

Perceptions are formed by the unique phenomenon of the mind. The mind works on the perceptions and then, the neural pathways that make the mind think are formed in the brain. The mind works like a supercomputer which continually creates thoughts, and these thoughts form a virtual world of their own.

Let us see how it works.

Consider this case scenario.

You see a woman shouting at her son.

What happens in your mind?

Your eyes and ears convey the sensations to your brain, and then your mind perceives the situation as good or bad, depending on your beliefs in the context of shouting.

If the mother is shouting because the son is not able to solve a simple mathematical question on addition, your mind may consider it good or bad, depending on your beliefs about strictness around teaching.

If your experiences as a child were bad because your mother or your father were really rough while teaching you, in every instance in your life where there is talk about teaching a child, your obsession will reflect in your behaviour, decisions, and actions.

Q: Isn't all thinking obsessive thinking, as thinking has to do with some or the other past experiences in life?

A: Not all thoughts are invasive. Only a few thoughts cause discomfort every time they appear. Most of your thoughts are obsessive in nature because you have fed them a lot of energy for a long time. You have facilitated the obsession by being very concerned about these thoughts.

An example of such a thought is, *'I am so vulnerable and people always cheat me.'*

You have believed it the first time your mind selectively assessed the people who cheated you. And who knows if those people cheated you or if you didn't set the rules well in advance and because of your carelessness, they deemed their benefits their rights.

We can compare this situation to another one.

On a dark night, I park my car irresponsibly, blocking the highway. A speeding car hits my car. I can easily blame the other person. Now, if I have a habit of putting the blame on others, every time I encounter a similar situation, I will be feeding energy to the thought that people are careless these days. Not realising that it was about me as well and merely a consequence of both my actions and the other party's actions that led to the particular situation.

Q: What is normal thinking, then?

A: It is not the coming of the thoughts, but thinking consciously that has to be stopped. Thoughts may come; and when you don't pay attention to thoughts, it can be said that you are not thinking.

For example, if the thought "It is too cold today" occurs to you, and you just don't indulge in the thought, the thought will subside. Even though it is a reality that it is a cold day, this reality will not impact you. But when you allow the mind to think, you will classify the coldness of the day as bad, and thereby, surely be impacted. Subsequently, the new thought that you willfully think is, "I hate winters." This will then turn into obsessive thinking.

Until the first thought "It is a cold day" occurred, it was just a thought. But when you think "I hate winters," you are creating an obsession, which then becomes your reality, rather a reality in your world, that is going to give you discomfort. This may not be a reality for others who don't think the same way. The day will still be cold for others. However, they are not uncomfortable because it is you who thinks negatively, not them.

Q: Does obsessive thinking impact our decisions?

A: Of course, obsessive thinking impacts our decision-making. The decision is influenced by our beliefs because we are bound to like or dislike situations, people, and things based on our beliefs. These biased decisions create our life.

Q: Can we ever get out of the habit of obsessive thinking and live freely?

A: Yes. All you need to do is to remember and practice to not think. This book has a well-researched, foolproof and time-tested way of 'not thinking.' The only pre-condition is to be committed to the purpose—to live freely. The technique is very simple, and it is practical as well.

Q: Will we become so free that we will completely stop working?

A: Nobody will stop something by merely reading a book. If the body is hungry, it will fetch food on its own. If the body is feeling cold, it will find a warm shelter on its own. Similarly, whatever the gross needs are, you will be working on them.

The only thing that will be different is you will be not tired, stressed, or obsessed. So you will not be consumed by the work, you will be living, and the work will be happening. Rather, you will get so much freedom that will create much better capabilities to complete all your life goals and aspirations.

CHAPTER *Three*

The Science Behind Boredom

If you often find yourself stung by this demon called 'boredom', this is something important for you. Leo Tolstoy referred to **boredom** as the *desire for desires*. If you closely observe it, you will be able to understand what he meant by this. When you indulge in thinking excessively about your desires— be it a new car, the latest bag collections, the home of your dreams, or your fantasy girl or guy, you are bound to get bored. This happens because you over-live an imaginary life that you want to live. Please note the two important words—**over-live** and **imaginary**.

When you imagine, you exhaust your mental energies and do not act through the body. This creates a conflict in the mind. If this is a continuous pattern of re-experiencing, and re-experiencing, and re-experiencing the frustration caused by living in your imagination, you are bound to get bored. These feelings of boredom tend to make you uninterested in everything. This makes you an interesting person, which further pushes away all your friends.

This is happening increasingly among the youth today. Boredom comes to those who take a break from their work schedules and rest. The best way that is taught to us, as kids, is to fill the gap by going for a movie, a holiday, or simply going out to eat. This complicates the mind even more because a day comes when you are bored of all these fillers as well, and you no longer enjoy dining at restaurants or holidays, rather, you bore those poor friends and family who go along with you.

Q: Have you ever thought why boredom happens to you?

A: It happens when you don't like what you are doing. Let me explain this differently. When you start disliking what you are doing; and when the importance of what you do diminishes in your mind, you start getting bored. It certainly doesn't mean that you should not think of growth. However, boredom occurs when you start thinking only about growth and not about what you are doing.

If you are bored of your car, it doesn't mean that getting a new car is going to make you happy forever. In fact, if you get a new car, you are certainly not working on the problem. The problem is in your mind and not the car. I don't say that you should not get a new car, but when you start disliking what you have, it is certain that it will only be a matter of time before you start disliking the new object that you get.

Isn't this a sort of an illness of the mind? Yes, it is.

Q: If boredom is an illness of the mind, can it be treated?

A: Boredom is an emotional state of displeasure and disinterest in the surroundings. Now, this is more likely to happen when the level of challenges given to someone is less compared to his or her abilities. It certainly doesn't mean that one should not work towards increasing one's abilities.

It is true that once when you overcome a set of challenges, they become unexciting for you. So if you are amongst those who are always on the chase for excitement, you are prone to have this illness, surely. The good news is that you can work on it.

The first step is to realise the root cause of boredom is not the lack of interest but the disliking. When you master your mind's disapproval of what *is*, you can train the mind to accept all that is, at this point in time. And at another point in time as well. And at yet another.

You are probably thinking that it is really difficult to accept the concept. It is true that it is difficult, but only until you find a way out. The solution is coming your way in this book soon.

Q: Can't we sometimes be bored in reality and may it not just be a fault in our thinking?

A: As you have just learnt, boredom is a reality only for those who are not able to accept the present and run behind more challenges that give more excitement. Isn't it like having a continual need to solve a tedious, time- consuming puzzle, as if you are addicted to the satisfaction you get from solving it, which is so impermanent and very short-lived?

Now every time you get bored, just check if you are satisfied with what is. Doing so, you will discover that this is like a pandemic that generations have been passing on to later generations.

Long ago, the wisdom of the Eastern World had discovered this truth— that life has to be lived just the way it is and one has to refrain from living a life of chasing. Even today, if you go to small villages of the countries in the east, you will find the older generation very content with what is.

Is such contentment very difficult to learn?

Q: Do you mean that all entertainment should be given up?

A: Certainly not. What I say is that when you are in front of the cinema screen, be a part of what is happening but don't be addicted to the thirteen-letter word 'entertainment' and bring bad luck to yourself.

If you don't believe this, you can try an experiment. Try watching five movies in a row on a single day. Repeat the same the next day, the day after that, and so on. If you can get rid of boredom, then, even continuously watching movies and sitting still in front of the screen won't make you weary.

Simply speaking, live through things as they happen. Even if there is a transition, it should be welcomed similarly without resistance.

Q: Isn't boredom a reason for the development of the new?

A: It is important to know the driving force behind any action. If you have started disliking something and that is why you have decided to escape and discover the new, it proves that there was no love and no life in the gone by, and it then becomes certain that there will be no love and life in the new as well. Surely, in such a case, you are in a chase and not *with* life.

Q: Should we live a renounced life? Isn't that too scary?

A: What is renunciation? Isn't that again a kind of running away? Here, you are learning to accept, rather, receive life the way it comes. So *being* in life is like enjoying and celebrating life. You will learn how to celebrate life in the coming chapters of this book.

CHAPTER *Four*

Compulsive Longing for Things

Q: Should one be satisfied with what one has, or should one get all that one can?

A: This is a question that has been posed across the ages. The compulsion to long endlessly has been ingrained in a newborn when the new parents talk to it saying, "You will grow up to be a great human."

Well, it is important to understand that the newborn itself is great as it is, in the present. It is a wonderful creation of nature. The credit, to induce the compulsion to long for something in the future, goes to the society and education that never teach beauty in the present form. There is an unconscious devaluation of the form of life in the present moment.

The eyes of the mind are always longing for something that is not there in the present. The *not wanting what you have* is the sole reason for this endless longing. The best part is that the value that is deemed in the object of longing is again very transient.

The moment the object is possessed, the value starts diminishing very quickly. The deeper reality is that the value is not in the desired object, it is in the mind of the person. The person adds coloured light of his own making to the neutral screen of the life.

And life itself is very neutral; it is only different people who see the same object differently.

A very simple example is that of a man who is selling his top branded car because of his longing for the latest high-end model which has just launched in the market. And the one who is buying the used car has a longing for that used car's brand. So although the car is the same, one has lost value for it in his mind and to someone else, it is a long-cherished, valuable possession.

Isn't it funny? What is funnier is that the story doesn't end here. The one who is buying the newly-launched higher-end brand new car model will quickly lose the interest in it after getting it. So the moment the object of desire is attained, the desire shifts to yet another unattained target. This is a madness of its kind in the mind.

Q: How will there be development in the world without longing for the better?

A: 'Not longing' doesn't mean that you stop working. Shunning the longing is to stop worrying. When the mind is worry-free, it will be able to freely do its task. The task of the mind is to create. Only in humans, this skill is highly developed, although several experiments have inferred that animals like dogs, rats, and even birds have a mind, which is why conditioning is possible.

Thanks to the family and society, a human baby is exposed to so much learning that develops the mind greatly. Now, one ill that comes through this learning is the craving for matter. There is a difference between craving for something and playing with matter like an artist.

For instance, consider how a painter plays with colours on the canvas. The artist doesn't have a craving; rather, he knows that whatever comes out is his expression, and he himself is not bothered about the source of his flow. He surrenders the *beingness* to the source and lets the creation happen on the canvas. So all he does is to provide an obstacle-free body to the source. And the world is able to see his creation. If you ask him, "Did you paint it?" he can never claim that it was he who painted it. And while the painting is happening, he is not thinking, longing, or anxious at all.

So the answer to the question is—yes, the world will be still in the process of making and developing as it always has been in the past and will always be in the future too. Whether you think or not, this has happened, it is happening now, and will continue to happen. So why do you need to unnecessarily think and long? All you need to do is to be like that free- minded painter and see the creation happening. With *Inner Self Integration*, you will learn how to be in that state.

Q: By not desiring, isn't one getting excused for not working?

A: The answer is already here in this present moment. Isn't the work still happening, right now?

The act of you reading this book is a work, and it has a purpose too. Similarly, at every point in time, there is some or the other work always. Work will always happen as long the mind exists. The mind is the creator.

Even if you sit idle and someone sees you, if that person is talking about you, he will say "he is sitting." So the verb 'sitting' in the statement also indicates an action that is happening. Not desiring is like not interfering in all that is happening around. And there is a valid objective, which is 'to live freely.'

The word 'living' itself is a verb and denotes the happening of an action. Living freely doesn't mean that you won't be working. You work but without having it impact your happiness and your liveliness.

You will learn some parts of the technique in your journey through this book, in the following chapters.

Q: When more than half the world has enough bread for their whole life, why do they still long for more?

A: Longing for more is a habit that everyone acquires from the society, right from the first day of consciousness. Every eye wants to see a perfect picture.

Who would not tell a child to write better, dance better, paint better, study better, and so on? Almost every parent inculcates an implied need for improved performance in the mind of a child.

Even though scriptures of all religions stress on 'Being happy with what has been given', you rarely find someone who is grateful and satisfied. The world can start changing only at one point —you.

Are you ready?

If the answer is 'Yes', you will learn some parts of the technique soon.

Q: If it was possible to get away from longing and craving, why has mankind not worked on it?

A: Mankind has worked on it several times. Whenever a war ends, the world comes to rest. A new life starts with all the good virtues. This doesn't mean war is needed for the occurrence of peace, it means that all the unrest leads to war. But the peace is possible only when all the causes behind the ill are well-identified. It is most important to realise the ultimate root cause behind all the wars in the history of mankind. It is greed.

There still exist places on earth, where people are content within themselves and with what all they have—you will find no war in such places. In places where there are less population and a relatively slower life, you will find less greed. Also, in such places, you will notice that people are relatively more religious compared to people in fast-life metros.

Q: So can the same learning be used to help people get rid of addictions, as addictions are also longings?

A: Indeed. What is an addiction? It is a dependency on any substance that impacts the functionality of any person. So the keyword to be noted is **dependency**. When people are dependent on any substance to get relief from an uncomfortable state, it is not about getting any sort of comfort, but getting rid of discomfort or fear.

There is no "fun" as such in any substance—be it alcohol or drugs. Before one indulges in alcohol, life is unaffected by it. But the first time one indulges, one feels differentness that one wants to experience again. This is, again, not a need but an aversion to the 'normal state' which takes the person into the 'high state.'

To explore the new is an inborn human tendency that may have had its origin in the monkey instincts.

But to get entrapped in the games of the mind is a choice. The choice is not about *not exploring* or stopping the movement of life. The choice is about being unbothered. Awareness about what needs to be learnt is also very important.

CHAPTER *Five*

Hurt Proneness of the Mind

Another peculiar characteristic of the mind is **'Hurt Proneness.'** The rising of emotions is a very normal mechanism that happens in the mind. Different emotions arise because of different incidents that happen in a day. Positive emotions arise when favourable situations happen, and negative emotions arise when there are unfavourable situations. Something that is favourable for you may be unfavourable for the other, and something that is unfavourable for the other may be favourable for you.

So whenever there is an unfavourable situation that seems to be created by the other, the mind experiences feeling hurt. Please observe that it only seems to be created by the other; in reality, it is a mere coincidence that the other appears as the creator to you. The other is not the creator; in fact, the other is also in the clutches of the mind, like you are. It is important to understand experience out of the three elements—the object, the subject, and the experience. The *object* being the incident, the *subject* being you, and the *experience* is the hurt.

Q: What is this hurt in reality?

It is merely a feeling. Note that the word 'feeling' is also a verb, which implies an unconscious action performed by your mind. Feeling hurt is about experiencing 'emotional suffering.' 'Emotions' is emoting what you learnt and is a normal phenomenon. But it is interesting to understand 'suffering' is at this point.

The word 'suffering' comes from the Latin word '*sufferre*' which means 'to carry.' This means if an incident has happened and you have experienced the momentary emotions, it is normal. But if the experience of emotions is carried by your mind long after the incident happened, then you are suffering. This indicates the auto functioning of the mind.

If you are asked a question, "Do you want to suffer?" your obvious reply will be "No, never." But still, you suffer. Yet this all happens, courtesy, your mind. Your mind is conditioned to feel hurt about a whole lot of things. It has been conditioned right from childhood.

Q: So is it the actions of the others or the mind that makes you suffer?

A: It is true that others just play their part in the story, but surely your mind makes you experience 'hurt' or 'suffering.' The good news is that this mind can be conditioned. If it could get conditioned then, it can be reconditioned again. This requires your connectedness to the objective which is to 'Be Happy' and mastery in the practice of some technique. The best part is that the technique is so simple that if you don't understand the base now, it will be too simple for your powerful mind to understand.

Q: Is it not normal to feel hurt?

A: Yes, it is normal for the mind to make you experience the hurt. But to continue to suffer from the feelings of hurt is a choice that you have. Now, when you know that it is possible to do away with the hurt, you need to be committed to your freedom, unlike all others who continue to live with a heavy load.

Q: Do you mean that we should live like vegetables, that anyone can come and hurt us?

A: Certainly not. In any case, all the events that happen, happen on their own, simply as a result of many factors. Someone acting unfavourably towards you is a result of many factors like his personality, his situation, the circumstance prevailing at a particular point in time, your vulnerability, and your unawareness of many facts.

Don't you find this these factors coincidental?

However, your mind finds a very easy route—that is to blame the other. There are two actions that you perform effortlessly. One at the mind level and the other, at the material level. You understand that the action at the mind level is just your mind's defence mechanism and a coping mechanism of your mind. This action brings you to a composed position that makes you capable of performing the required action at the material level well. The action at the material level centers on performing the corrective action from your end.

Q: Can mind be conditioned to not feel hurt?

A: It is not about not feeling hurt. Instead, it is about learning to live free. As explained earlier, hurt is normal but freedom is an attitude. It is a way of *being*, which is based on a conscious choice. Slowly, with practice, a day comes when people comment that you don't get hurt no matter what. You will not be able to realise that state because you will be in that state.

Q: To what extent will be able to maintain our calm and not feel hurt?

A: Once again, please understand you don't need to suppress the hurt. You need to shift the focus to freedom. It is like you have a choice to be in the darkness, which doesn't exist in itself. It is simply the absence of light. Merely choosing to be the light will solve your problem.

Being in darkness is being without light. And being in the light is being without darkness. There is nothing in the middle. So whenever the darkness appears, remember that you forgot to be the light.

CHAPTER *Six*

The Mind's Habit of Thinking Short of Self

A strange fact is that inferiority is only learnt by humans. Do you find animals or plants that feel inferior? Feeling inferior happens because the mind compares the self as lesser than the other. It wouldn't have happened if the other people didn't feed this into the mind of the child. The sense of inferiority is a disease that is passed on from one generation to the next. Isn't this sad? But it is so true.

Weren't you taught right in childhood—this is good and this, bad? All these distinctions have created this *dis-ease* of the mind. It is very rare to find people who don't compare. Being fulfilled and complete is the truth. The universe is designed that way. Look at the earth—it is complete in itself, and yet, connected to the sun and space (where it moves). Look at the sun— complete in itself, but connected to the gambit of millions of stars in the galaxy and space (where it moves).

But beyond all these realities, the mind finds itself inferior. You were very much made capable, capable for a simple purpose—survival. And you were endowed with a mind, unlike the animals.

This mind had beautiful capabilities like remembering things, analysis, comparison, etc. But weren't these capabilities intended for the core purpose of survival? Look at the beauty of nature—when it saw that the mind was using these capabilities for a negative cause, i.e., against humanity, nature made the mind work against the self.

Thus, the mind started thinking negatively about the body and fellow beings. Doesn't your mind make judgements about your own self and fellow humans? These judgements generally have a negative connotation. Either the mind thinks short of the self or short of others around. This, in social sciences, is termed 'self-Esteem.'

Self-esteem is the estimate of the *self*. Have you ever thought how your mind thinks about or estimates your *Self*, i.e., you as an individual? A large percentage of people have a negative belief about themselves that they CANNOT handle life's problems. It is the mind. Their mind also adds a lot of negative adjectives to define their *self*.

Some of the common statements that people may think of are—

I can never....

I am not worthy to them that's why they... I am not perfect in...

I shouldn't have...

I am not good enough Nobody loves me

The list goes on.

Doesn't your mind also say some of these statements often? Yes, it does.

This is the critical mind that always makes you feel short of yourself.

Q: Have you ever wondered where this critical mind is coming from?

A: It started from childhood. Right after the first month of your birth, when you did something against the wish of your parents, they criticised you with statements like, "*Why are you making noise*", "*You should not have you done this*", "*Are you crazy?*" and so on.

Since then, if you believe you have done anything in a way that is expected, your mind starts voicing similar statements on its own. Funny! Isn't it? You know it is not your parents' fault either; even you criticise your children, or family, or friends or anyone who doesn't do things your way.

Isn't this like an inheritance that has been passed down by generations of minds to the ones that followed? This is how your mind now works so efficiently. The moment something is done different from the status quo, your mind itself reprimands you by criticising or thinking negatively about your being.

The big question that arises is **Can the critical mind be stopped?**

The answer is 'Yes.'

This book has chapters coming up that will help you learn a very simple way of creating a positive self-esteem.

Q: If we just see the positives about ourselves, will we not be fooling ourselves and living in darkness?

A: One needs to be careful of the trap of the critical mind. There is a difference between the scope of growth and criticism, and making one feel short of self. For most people, the mind behaves like a critic who has to put the *self* down when an undesired situation arises.

Life will always have two forms like day and night, winter and summer because as Science describes, change is a fundamental truth. Relativity is another fundamental truth—the interconnectedness. So there will be situations of loss and gain in human life.

The mind has a habit of holding one's own self responsible for all occurences. If there is a gain, the mind will say 'I gained this', but is it actually true? Were there not hundreds of other coinciding factors that were responsible for that gain? Similarly, when there is a loss, there are so many factors responsible for the loss.

The mind, because of childhood conditioning (the *dis-ease*), holds you solely accountable for the loss. On the contrary, if the mind doesn't play the role of a critic, you will have a much better possibility of discovering the best course of action for any situation at hand.

Q: Is it about accepting our weakness? How will we improve our skills and strengths then?

A: Certainly not. It is not the acceptance of weakness. It is the elimination of the word 'weakness.' This book will help you identify and correct the criticising nature of the mind and make you capable of taking the necessary actions.

You need to see the goodness first, and then you can talk about creation. The only truth is energy as studied in Science. There is energy (matter) and space. There is no third thing.

The world is a play of energy and space. There is no third thing. But there is a mind as well. This mind too is energy. Now, how it plays is a question. Can it play the way it should? Yes.

For that, you need to know how to make the mind play to your advantage, instead of being played by the mind. The mind can be compared a robot. If you feed wrong data into it, it will wrong everything. But if you put the right data in the mind, it will serve its best to the master—you.

Q: How can we think good about the self and also increase our capabilities?

A: The first step is to know that you are good. For this, you need to know who you are in reality—your existence. Subsequently, your mind will feel good about your existence. You will not have to forcibly tell your mind to feel good about the self. And then, as mentioned earlier, you will clearly see the action that needs to be done. All you need to learn is about your own self and then, practice the learning.

Q: Should we just reject people who give us negative feedback?

A: The negative is unawareness, not the people. One who clearly distinguishes this achieves liberation from the trap of the mind. The negative can be. Perhaps there is no such thing as negative. It is the absence of the positive, the absence of truth.

The rejection of unawareness has to happen and happen only in your own self, not in the other. There is no other but a reflection of you. You have allowed all the negative in the other to happen. You will learn more of this later in the book.

CHAPTER *Seven*

Self-Pressure Because of Life Goals

This is the biggest and the most powerful trap of the mind—*Life Goals.* Have you ever thought of the sun's goal? Does the sun keep a track of the goal? Are you aware that the whole solar system runs because the sun plays its role? Hence, it plays its role for the earth and all the life on earth. Does the sun evaluate its performance and live under pressure? Do the mountains, the river, and the oceans review their life goals? The human mind has been trained from generation to generation to emphasise this ongoing pressure called **Life Goals**.

Humanity, as a life form, is provided with the best of abilities compared to all other life forms. Because of the mind, humans can survive well, compared to other animals. Humans can rule over the whole earth, unlike animals. Humans are the only life form that can even go outside the atmosphere and travel into space. The sad part is that due to this ability, this mind shifted its focus from 'living' to 'achieving.' This shift has led to diseases like depression, self-harm, harm to others, etc. The mind can be used for better causes as well.

It's so funny that something that was an advantage has become a disadvantage. Is it the mind or the information fed to the mind? The mind is a neutral tool like a knife. A knife is an advantage when you have to cut open a fruit. The same knife is a disadvantage if a burglar fetches it from your kitchen to get his money. Who is this deluded burglar running around clueless, playing a negative role? It is the mind. A burglar also has the same talent as a scientist.

Both are finding and achieving something. But taking opposite directions takes them to different destinations. So is this mind which is talented, but works against us. It exerts so much pressure to achieve life goals. There is a difference between performing a task under pressure and performing a task effortlessly. It is possible to work on the mind and then use the mind to create a meaningful life effortlessly.

It's only knowledge and practice that can make you recondition your mind to live effortlessly. Knowledge has to be really simple and should produce an immediate result. Only then, the mind can get convinced to adopt the new way. Some parts of the technique mentioned in the book are so simple and get you immediate results that will instantly help you achieve a state of effortless living and craft a meaningful life.

Q: Should one have no life goals?

A: Having life goals is different from achievements being the purpose of life. Doing something productive in an organised manner is normal, in fact, good. But living lifelessly like a machine is a disease that humanity has acquired due to the mind's unawareness.

Goals that are made by the mind are limited because the maker of those goals—the mind itself—is limited, limited to the level of awareness. The mind doesn't know anything beyond the limited world that it sees and compares itself with. All the creative people—artists, scientists, architects, etc—cross the limit of the mind and think beyond it. If asked, "Where did the idea come from?" they cannot reply to the question. They will also not be able to answer the question, "Did you come up with the idea?" correctly. Their reply will certainly be, "The idea came to my mind."

The mind is a door to the beyond if connected well. Only an aware mind can connect to the beyond. A person whose mind has a lot of ego (i.e., limitation to the self) cannot attain its full potential. Even the person with ego feels proud about some achievement that has happened. However, he mistakenly and unknowingly claims the achievement as his.

There are millions of causes that coincide to make the achievement or event happen. But the unaware gets into the trap of the ego. Investing energy in maintaining a stand requires or consumes a lot of mental energy (or pressure on self) that could have been used to create something else.

With time, if more achievements happen and the mind begins to feel that it has achieved so much on its own, it creates a larger version of this self-pressure, also known as **Life Goals**. Your whole life is then consumed by this pressure to achieve these goals. You miss out on life because of this chase.

Q: How is a life of effortlessness different from the life that everyone is living in the present times?

A: Most people live life as if it were a task, as if it is a duty that they have to fulfil. Do the plants, flowers, and the birds live like that? They live free. Rather, they just live. They go with the need of the moment. They probably do not even realise the need. They may be working, not knowing that they are working. But humans live with a continuous, never-ending pressure on their head around the life goals. The funniest part is that this pressure is yielded by their own mind. No newborn is given a list of life goals at the time of birth. But the society, which is a collection of millions of minds, trains the mind of a child from the age of three to become something or do something when he or she grows up.

Another funny thing is that whenever you meet a friend after a long time, he or she will ask you "What are you doing these days?" They expect a reply around your life goals. This is like a communicable *dis-ease*. They transfer this *dis-ease* to you, and you transfer the same to them. The compulsion to answer this question has created this term called 'Stress.' Animals have no such thing.

All the tasks necessary for maintaining a good life can be performed without putting in so much effort. There are simple techniques to do away with this pressure or the habit of getting pressurised. What is the compulsion to raise the target over and over again in the mind and living a life of continuous pressure? This discipline is a default in animals. The birds don't fetch food after the sun sets. The lion doesn't eat more than the stomach needs, it doesn't even hunt if it is not hungry. It is still a lion.

Humans who are most intelligent amongst the life forms are the dumbest in this regard. Humans have the best of the intellect to get food. But it is the fear of future and the comparative image that make them form life goals. Living a meaningful life is different from a life of chasing materialism. At the same time, it is important to use the materialism as a medium to add meaning to life. Living a purposeful life is different from running behind aspirations and self-pressurising desires of tomorrow.

Q: Is effortlessness not shirking our responsibilities?

A: Effortless living is all about living and not living with effort. It is doing the same thing seamlessly. If you are a master of some art or some skill, look at the way an artist creates the art. The artist simply lets the art flow through his or her hands. The artist cannot declare that he or she has created the art. Art flows through the artist. This happens only when the artist lets the art flow. This state is effortless when the artist becomes a pure, clean desireless channel. He or she connects the self so much with the equipment. This is effortlessness.

There are a few people who dissolve their ego and then work effortlessly. This is the reason they are able to fulfil their responsibility so efficaciously. When the person knows that he and only he is responsible, he doesn't find himself different from the task. The task and he become one, and at this state, he doesn't have to put in any effort.

Effort is required when a task is done forcefully and when the person knows he will get something out of the task. As a result, the task is done thinking about the outcome. This is a transactional act, and so will involve effort. But when there is no deal but pure oneness with the task, where it is done without expectation, the action happens *from* the self and *for* the self. This is effortless action.

Of course, the third person can say that an action is happening and a responsibility is being fulfilled. The doer will not even know that there is a responsibility. That task is an obvious and default task for the doer.

Q: Isn't self-pressure good to achieve a secured life for ourselves and our family?

A: Securing life for one's self and family is an obvious task any person has to do. But doing the needful happily and effortlessly is possible. Some people get so obsessed with acquiring wealth and things for the family that they forget the objective. The object becomes the objective. If the family members are asked, they are probably using the wealth and the goods, but even they carry unhappy faces.

Wealth is good and should be earned but enjoyed as well. This will happen when there is joy in earning wealth and the objective of being with family while enjoying the wealth is diligently remembered. People who are obsessed with working and amassing wealth are always asked questions such as "What have you done for us?" by their family members. The truth is that self-pressure will lead to frustration, which is projected on the people closest to you.

Working with pressure and obsession will yield the output wealth but also create issues with health and family relations. Therefore, it is the pressure and not the wealth that brings adverse consequence. Working objectively yields the same financial output when compared to working obsessively. In addition, the love and affection from the family will add to the energies and increase mental capability, thereby yielding more financial gains.

CHAPTER *Eight*

The Rat in the Rut

A rut is a sunken track or groove or furrow made by the passage of people or vehicles. Here the use of the word 'rut' implies a narrow or predictable way of life, a set of attitudes, or an undeviating routine.

A rat is always restless and preoccupied. A rat can never be seen calm until it is dead. What is it that the rat is occupied with, and why is it so occupied? Is it that the rat doesn't know that there could be another way? Is it that it would be an effort to explore the new way, or is it completely beyond his thinking because it has been in a rut right from the beginning?

The answer to all these questions is very simple, but your mind may rebel. This is the biggest trap of the mind. Leaving old patterns is easy and can happen in a second, but the decision happens only when the mind allows a new reality in.

The rut in the mind is the hunt for something that nobody is able to see. Sometimes, you may feel that you are living a fixed, monotonous life. But again, when the new day begins, the mind puts you back in the rut. The mind always feels that there is something less, but it is never able to fill that something less. It is always wishing for a life that it will live or wants to live.

Ask anyone, "When will you be happy?"

You will get an answer that goes – "I will be happy if I get a......"

But do you think that person will be happy for more than a month if he or she gets that......?

Certainly not.

The mind is always longing for things, like a greedy squirrel (a rat family rodent) who wants to collect the maximum number of nuts and save them, but does the day ever come when the squirrel enjoys the nuts?

The funny reality is that the squirrel sows the nut in the mud, and the nut disappears and turns into a plant. This plant will be of no use for this squirrel but will bear hundreds of nuts for the squirrels of the future.

Couldn't that first squirrel take the learning and pass it on to future generations? There is indeed a solution to this trap of the mind.

The technique is very simple. More than the technique, it is about knowing a truth. The truth is very simple. At the same time, it is too simple for the mind to accept. You need to be very open to the truth, only then you will be able to get liberated from all these traps of the mind. The moment the truth sinks in your mind, you will feel the liberation and start a new life where you live, and there will be no rut and no rat, but life. You will see life flowing.

Life is about the experience, not the object. It is obvious that if objects are there, the experience will be different. To experience is a skill. The differentness of the experience should not become the purpose of life. The purpose of life should be to experience life and not to create a differentness of experience. Because then, you miss out on the objective. The mind has been conditioned such that it moves in this rut of creating a set experience.

The rut is that wealth, name, and fame should be created as if you are a wealth-creating machine. Your life will go on in this rut unless you get out of the rut. Your mind may argue that if you do not walk on this rut, it is very risky for survival. This is untrue. The mind will, in any case, make the body work towards earning money and getting things of comfort. But if you come out of the 'rut means' where you are not a wealth-creating machine, but you also earn money, you do a good work of value addition in whatever work you do. The only difference is that you are not dependent on things and situations to be happy.

But as mentioned earlier, to be happy, is a skill. The book has a section for the stage when you are ready to receive the skill.

Q: Aren't all humans in this rut?

A: Indeed, all humans are in the rut. And as all of them are in the rut, none of them realise they are in a rut. This is so because there is no comparison. In a way, everybody is unaware. Most people live a very monotonous life that has very little meaning. They appear to be working towards their illusionary dreams which are endless. They are never fulfilled. These people appear to be moving, but in reality, they are not able to catch their dreams, ever.

In simple words, they always remain where they are, because their dreams are always distant because of the changeability of the target dream. The best part is that very few get to know that they are in the rut, and none of these people know how to get out of the rut.

Still, knowing you are in the rut is the first step. This is a fortunate state to be in. At least now, you can find out the further steps.

Q: Isn't this coming out of the rut, going take away the taste from life? Will life not be boring?

A: The bigger question that you need to ask yourself is, "Have you ever tasted life?"

You run from one taste, of this material world, to another. But you have never allowed your mind to immerse itself in the taste of the experience of life. In fact, the present way of living is anxious living.

But if you really learn to get out of the rut, you will taste the beyond for the first time, and it will be unique. You may fall so in love with that taste that there will be no going back. Leaving the monotonous chase is much more boring than learning to taste life as it appears. The book will uncover the specific way to develop this mind skill.

Q: Will a person who comes out of the rut become a saint?

A: This is a common fear that most people have when anything related to spirituality is introduced for the first time. The fear is that one needs to leave the worldly business, involvement, family, and refrain from any sort of entertainment. People who do not have any awareness about spirituality fear that a saint has to leave everything and go sit on top of a hill, away from everything and everyone. You too may have a similar image of people who are truly spiritual.

All religions were constituted to inculcate the right way of living. Even the word 'religion' comes from the words 'to rely'. Religions are just sets of faiths and beliefs that one can rely on. But do these religions talk about leaving everything? No. After all, even if one leaves everything, he or she will create discomfort. Discomfort to the self, to the family, to people who are dependent on them. So living in a right, balanced way is the objective. Living free and a living a fulfilled life is the goal. One need not leave anything.

Also, it is important to understand what the word 'saint' means. A saint is a person who is holy. The word 'saint' comes from the Latin word *sanctus* which means 'to concentrate.' According to this meaning, a saint is one who concentrates. He is not a person who needs to leave the worldly life. To be a saint means to concentrate on what is true and not just be blown away with what is not true. Going ahead, in *Inner Self Integration*, you will learn the way to effectively deal with any situation that disturbs you.

Q: Isn't leaving this worldly life the only solution to coming out of the rut?

A: Again, being an escapist is not the solution. If it was, all the population of the world will get atop the mountains. What then? It will create the same problem there. People will keep leaving the place. Then, there will be nobody on any part of the earth. This is useless thought, but good entertainment for the mind. Running away—where? Can you run away from the self? After all, the thoughts are in the mind. Nothing and nobody can actually disturb you.

It is your mind that thinks, and it is your mind that leads to emotions that you feel in your heart. The others just do the action, and those actions are just the interplay of so many things, so many situations that are bound to happen as long as you are alive. But how your mind interprets and thereby, how you feel is something that you need to focus on and work on. Now you may wonder why you should only work on the self. Even if you say so, in the end, the right action will come only through you. You will learn all the steps in detail.

PART *Two*

Are You Just Your Name

If you are asked *"Who are you?"* your answer will obviously be your name. This is obvious for all practical purposes. But a 'name' is a just a word used to describe some entity. This word helps in distinguishing one entity from other entities. So are you just that word with a few letters, or are you that entity? If you are just your name, you need to check this out. This may appear a bit funny or weird, but it is serious. If you are further asked, "If you are not your name, then who are you?" your reply will be "I am a body." Perhaps you will state your gender as well, something like this—"I am a man or woman." Yet, this is just the description of the gender of the body.

Are you just your body? If you are just the body, then when the body dies, where do you go? To this, your answer will be—"When the body goes, I also go." Isn't it? Now this means that you are the body also. Rather, you exist through the body. And here is a turning point with the big question—"Who am I"? Humans have struggled with this question since early man started thinking thousands of years ago. Interestingly, the moment you find the answer to this question, all your troubles will disappear. Isn't that funny? That you have been living for so many years now and you are living unconscious of your own existence. So who are you living for, who have you been fighting for, whom have you been wanting things for?

Most people when asked such questions, find it really irritating, some even find it annoying. And then they reply in a very self-protecting way like, "All this is *non-sense*!" Indeed, it is *non-sense* because they are not able to derive any sense in it. It is because they are unaware and feel scared of handling this untaught truth. Most so-called masters of religion themselves were never aware of this truth. If they were, even they would have gotten liberated. The truth should always liberate and not bind. If the truth liberates the person from misery, it is the truth, else it is a bondage.

And as the word 'religion' comes from a Latin word that means 'to rely', people should be able to rely on the truth. The religion must be able to liberate people and not bind, in terms of mere rituals and discipline. The right master must be able to bring out the truth and promote people to observe some principles and beliefs that liberate people from misery. The first step is to start our journey towards liberation from the misery of everyday life, by first understanding "who we are."

Q: Does that mean I should stop calling myself by my name or even refer to myself by my gender?

A: Of course, the aim is not to confuse you with your name. This concept is to know the True Self, and there is a clear purpose behind it. When you relate yourself to the transactions of the world, then your assessment of the self is dependent on the transactions of the world. The Science of psychology terms it "Self-Esteem."

Simply speaking, as of now, your self-esteem depends on how people treat you and how much you are valued in the world. You feel good if people treat you well or when they acknowledge you for your achievements. You feel bad when they don't treat you as you expect them to treat you. This self-esteem impacts your emotional state as well.

What if you have a positive self-esteem that is independent of people and transactions with the world?

This is possible with *Inner Self Integration*, and you will get there.

Q: How will my real life problems end by understanding who I am? A: When you know your Real Self, you will relate yourself with that True Self.

This will be done using the mind. The mind will get the attention in that reality and not the transient (changing) reality of life's everyday incidents. You will have to consciously train the mind towards that direction. And with practice, in a few days, your response to any situation will be in accordance to that Real Self of yourself.

In other words, you will be operating from a newer perspective. This new perspective will help you distinguish yourself from the scene or the people involved. This way, you will be out of the cloud of emotions that trap you. And you will find it really easy to perceive the situation in the right way and thereafter, take the needed steps that will be effective. This way, all life problems will be a matter of merely a simple decision that your new rational mind will take.

Q: Will I have to alter the religious beliefs that I follow?

A: Not at all. You will be rather astonished when you understand that your religious practice actually meant the same. The rights and rituals will make sense to you when you understand the logic behind them. You will be able to better relate to your religion when you know your Real Self.

All religions talk about the truth and when you experience the truth yourself, you appreciate your religion more. If it is the truth, it obviously must be universal; otherwise, it is not the truth. It can't be untrue in one religion and true in the other.

Inner Self Integration in no way alters, interferes with any religion or faith but simply talks about liberation and free living. You create a life full of freedom from misery, sorrow, any difficulty of the mind, and any real life concern.

Q: How will I co-exist with my people who won't understand this?

A: You will continue living the way you have been living all this while, amongst your people in your world. The difference will be that you will start getting compliments about the freshness in your life, your resilience, and the smile on your face. Of course, don't attempt to teach, explain in detail, or convince anyone.

You may simply recommend *Inner Self Integration* to them in case they want to. This new way of life will help you to better understand the people around you. You will start dealing with them in the right way, and you will be able to establish deeper relationships with all those who are close to you.

CHAPTER *Nine*

The Wrong Notions About Your Identity

Identity is being a person. It is how you see yourself and how you want the world to see you. It's funny that the first statements that are fed to a child who is barely a few months old are—"You must grow up to become a big man or a very beautiful, elegant woman." Adjectives such as 'big', 'beautiful', 'elegant' form a compulsive pressure that revolves in almost everyone's minds.

This compulsive need to be *someone* pushes one to hold on to a particular identity, beyond which, it is impossible to see. It is a web that doesn't allow one to think anything else. All through life there is an invisible pressure to create and carry that identity. This identity with the body ends after years of continued struggle. It can also be described as a compulsive sense to be somebody. Again, if you are asked the question "Who are you?" your answer will be a function of this identity that you carry. It's like an imaginary world that you have built unknowingly all around you, and you will die with this world you have built. Who knows, it may go along with the body in the next birth as well, if there is a next life.

There is a normal sense of ego or identity that one needs to carry to be functional or operational in this world. Of course, it is needed for all practical purposes. At the same time, it creates a very limiting, stereotypical role you have to live through to meet the expectations of the self, which is simply not needed. This pressure encloses you in a 'thinking trap' and doesn't allow you to see all the wholesomeness that life offers. Instead, you end up being consumed with a single cause that was valid, but not everything. People end up damaging their relationships, health, and sanity owing to this conditioning.

Q: Do I have to leave this identity? If so, should I stop what I am doing? What will I do for a living, then? Or how will I fulfil my responsibilities?

A: It is not the identity that you have to leave. It is the obsession with this identity that you have to leave. The obsession leads you to act in ways that take you deeper into the compulsion to live a controlled life. It is funny that you are trapped and the belief inside your own mind is the trap. Finally, this identity is just the belief that this is all you are.

There is a lot more to life that you need to figure out, apart from the role (i.e., the identity) you play to make a living or in your relationships. Leaving this role or not performing your responsibilities will further add to the complication in the mind. You will end up feeling even worse.

Your obsession with this role creates unnecessary stress in your life. So the solution is to perform these roles and experience the precious life that you have, that you are unaware of. This life is the existence that will be discussed in *Inner Self Integration*.

Q: Isn't everybody caught in this identity trap?

A: Yes! This is how it is meant to be. This is perfect too. Humans were given this extra intelligence—the mind which had the power to think. The power to think deeper. The power to reason. The power to find out the reasons. The power to connect the dots and discover.

Unfortunately most—if not all—just get used to using their mind to amass, to possess things. Almost everyone wants to become complete by accomplishing things and acquiring positions. And to this end, they end up struggling. Some may gain exactly all that they aspire, some may gain half of what they aspire, and some don't gain. But in the long run, all are in despair.

The ones who gain all that they aspire lose interest the minute they arrive at *consumption* or *possession*. For example, the new car, the new home, or the new brand of clothing loses its charm leading to the next pursuit. And then to the next, and to the next, and so on. This is despair. Those who achieve half of their pursuits and those who don't achieve are in despair anyhow.

All three categories of people use their minds to move through the journey, only to eventually arrive at despair. This doesn't mean people should stop achieving or working. Each one should earn his or her bread and create comfort for his or her family. But you should be aware of the unconscious use of the mind that creates the rat race. You must perform your responsibilities and continue your pursuits but do it effortlessly, as if this is also a part of the whole.

The mind can be used to discover the truth and liberate itself from this myopic trap. The phenomenon is like that of a camera focussing on its object, rendering the objects in the background not as sharply visible. Similarly, your eye can see the larger image behind. Similarly, the larger is not visible if one just focuses on the limited. Of course, the mind has this capacity, and this is the illusion.

At every point in time, either the larger or the limited is visible. The limited includes your name, gender, and your role. And the larger is *the you* beyond all this. It is only the awareness of *the you* beyond that will liberate you from everyday stress and despair. And thereon, you will live and find yourself fulfilling your everyday pursuits with greater satisfaction and joy.

Q: How does one live a life in totality?

A: A life of totality is one where you are present and not absent. This is a state where you are not continually obsessed to be someone (identity).

To live in totality is about being in awareness and in a state where you cherish all the incidents happening around you and inside you. Here, you don't judge anything as good or bad. You live in complete awareness and the acceptance of things happens both outside your body and inside of your mind.

The more you understand the concept of "Self" in *Inner Self Integration*, the clearer this will become. This life of totality is full of joy, newness, and a sense of feeling complete. Yet, this is a knack you will only achieve when you thoroughly know the technique of *Inner Self Integration*.

Q: Will I not become non-serious if I am casual about my identity?

A: Being in totality is not being non-serious. There is a difference between being serious, being fearful, being anxious, being preoccupied, and being joyful. Being joyful is not about concentrating less on work when you are at work. However, you will be more attentive at work if you are living a full life.

For example, if you are completely enjoying your food while eating, fully enjoying nature while walking in the park, or even fully immersed in music when listening to the song that you like, you will be able to be fully attentive and perform your work.

Even if you are a mom who does not work for money but as a homemaker, your identity is not only 'a homemaker.' You are beyond that as well. You will be able to care for the home better if you are not obsessed. The responsibility will not be a burden; rather, it will be a source of enjoyment.

CHAPTER *Ten*

Demystifying the Trap of Feelings

Feelings, as explained earlier in the book, are the mind's medium of communication. It is feelings that convey that you did something that you were not supposed to do. They also convey that you didn't do what was supposed to be done. Only those who are unaware and unable to grasp the signals that feelings emit are caught in the trap of feelings. And as a result, they keep flowing in the river of feelings.

Feelings are like the turbulent flow of a river. If you are dropped in the river, its powerful flow will draw you deeper and further away from where you were initially dropped. The river will never end if you don't do something about it. And if you don't understand the flow and get scared and reactive (the chances of which are really high), you may drown.

- The first step is to **realise that this has happened**. Whenever you experience a flow of emotions because of an unwanted situation, just be aware that you are feeling that emotion. For example, if you are angry, be aware that you are angry.
- The next level of awareness is one where you **realise the presence of the emotion**. For example, 'There is anger.' Now, this is the first step towards demystification – the awareness that there is anger. Similarly, if you have disgust or fear or sadness,

just sense that 'There is disgust' or 'There is fear' or 'There is sadness.' This separates the feeling and you; it tells you that you are different from your feeling. This works like magic because it in a way gives you control of the situation. When you have the control, you need to take the next step.

- The next step is to **be deeply aware of the source of the feeling**. The source of the feeling is not from the situation that has occurred or the person that was part of the situation. These are just the objects or characters in the movie. These characters are in the play or act, whereas the feeling arises in you. Your mind generates the feeling to tell you something, something that you were not aware of until now—"You did something that was not supposed to be done or you didn't do what was supposed to be done."

You can discover the message by connecting to the *Inner Self*. With *Inner Self Integration*, you not only get access to the immense knowledge that lies hidden in your *Inner Self* and gets you in charge of the situation and your feelings, it also helps you develop the capability to turn things around positively and in your favour.

Q: How can I be happy throughout the day? Is it practical and possible?

A: It is important to know what your definition of happy is. Is it carrying a smile on your face the whole day?

Or is it being excited, chirpy, and bubbly the whole day? This technique brings you to a state of joy—a state of being unaffected. This was well described by Lord Buddha as *adukha*. *Adukha* is derived from the word *dukha* that means misery. The absence of misery is joy. You can reach the state of joy if you practice *Inner Self Integration*.

Excitement and enthusiasm are emotions similar to dullness. These emotions change like the weather; they are just a consequence of the transactions that happen throughout your day. Some transactions trigger enthusiastic emotions and some, dull emotions. Emotions are bound to be triggered and appear just like the rainbow. The colours of the rainbow already exist but appear white and neutral. A particular colour may be visible when the light passes through a prism-like object. It is important to remember that light may look neutral; however, it is the source of life and that of the whole universe.

As great scientists have acknowledged, everything is made up of light. Here, being in the state of the ultimate, the true, and the unaffected doesn't mean that the different emotions will not appear. They will. How quickly you sense them, how quickly you connect to the *Inner Self*, how quickly you discover the source, and how quickly you act in accordance will make you arrive at that state of joy.

This is practical because *Inner Self Integration* is a simple step-by-step process. It has worked for thousands, and it will work for you because it is based on a fundamental principle that has to work with everyone.

Q: There are a few people who are a part of my life, and I can't get away from them. They are the source of my unhappiness and stress. How will my feelings of despair go away if they are around?

A: When a person cannot be the source of happiness, how can he or she be the source of unhappiness? The false sense of identity is. If someone has made you feel unhappy, look back carefully at your day.

Now say this statement aloud, *"I felt hurt by this person because he did ______ to me or said_to me."*

Now ask yourself, *"How can a person do___or say_ to anybody?"*

Just observe yourself. Aren't you in denial?

Aren't you holding beliefs that this can't be done or that can't be said?

Now answer yourself, *"Yes! Somebody can do this to somebody and somebody can say this to somebody. It is possible."*

Anyway, this has already happened, and it can happen.

What if you saw from a distance that somebody said something to somebody or did something to somebody? You would not feel good, but it would not have mattered to you. You would be able to get to the next level, which is identifying the reasons for it. There will certainly be a reason for it. What do you think could probably be the reason for this person's reason behind doing that or saying that? Now, you have built yourself up to a state where you are at least attempting to see the reality behind-the-scene.

You, thereafter, become wiser and arrive at working out the solution to the actual reality that is hidden—hidden behind the clouds of feelings. This is the trap of feelings that you can wipe out with *Inner Self Integration*. Of course, then your focus will shift from being a victim or being trapped with these people to working out the problem. But you certainly need practice. Thereafter, you neither long to run away nor continue to feel miserable being with these people who matter and who impact your life. You would rather quickly develop good working relationships with them, if not amazing relationships.

Q: If I stop having any feelings, will I not become insensitive?

A: It is not insensitivity, rather, being sensitive to emotions that form within. The technique builds your ability to sense the rise of an emotion and thereafter find the root cause and finally work on the cause. This way, you don't continue to be swayed in the river of emotions, or maybe drown and get consumed by the emotions. You will be able to be in charge of your emotions by working on the situation in the most balanced way and that too, effortlessly. You will be wiser and more compassionate. Not at all insensitive.

Q: If I don't feel and get in charge of my feelings, won't everybody get in control of my life? Will the wrongdoers not get more power when I become non-reactive?

A: Once again, you will feel the emotions, but with a difference—that you will be aware that you are feeling. This will build up your capacity to do something about the situation in a more effective manner. When I say effective, it means you will create a different effect by acting on the right (needed) response coming through your *Inner Self*. Your *Inner Self* has all the knowledge and brilliance to solve any challenging situation. It is the trap of the mind that labels people and situations as negative.

By not being aware of these behind-the-scene mechanics, you are choosing to add power to the doing. Your mind terms *the doing* the *wrongdoing* and the *doer* the *wrongdoer*. This is a trap—a trap that holds your intellect to find the solution (the right response) to the situation. *Inner Self*

Integration by no means teaches you to become suppressed, inactive, or sacrificing. It rather teaches you to act and not react. Not reacting is a power. Responding comes from this power of not reacting. Reacting is a combination of 'Re' and 'Acting.' This comes from old English— Repeating the Act.

So if someone has done wrong to you, you either let the wrong happen or you do similar or bigger wrong to the other. Both ways, you create a certain wrong consequence for yourself. With *Inner Self Integration*, you see the incident as it is and get that little time in between to see all of this. This gives you the much needed capacity to discover the best move in the given circumstance. But all this needs a good understanding of the concept and continuous, effortless practice.

CHAPTER *Eleven*

Attachment to the Body Sense

The minute you were born, you were simply considered a person, a body. And when they started addressing you as a person, by a name, an identity, you also developed the same belief. The biggest impact of this association with the identity is the association with the body. This is quite obvious because everybody doesn't have all this awareness that you have received up till now. So if anything happens to the body, all the people around you say that it has happened to you. For example, if you got a scratch on the skin on your hand while playing, your folks said, "Oh, you are hurt." That was where the trouble started. The body was hurt, not you. But you were not aware, and you also picked it up from there.

This is not the case with animals. They don't associate the self with the body. Now you will probably say they protect themselves, and they cry when they are hurt. These are normal mechanisms that happen in the body. But look at them, they are much more resilient. When they are under threat of being eaten by a predator, their body senses it and generates an adrenalin rush, and the body gets into the fight-or-flight response. It is all biology.

The interesting fact to note here is that it is the action of the body, not theirs. They don't keep thinking and feeling depressed much ahead of time like humans. They live real-time, unlike human beings. They don't keep worrying about the future. They don't have depression or low feelings or jealousy. Their body may have some pain, but they don't suffer. Suffering is carrying the pain in the mind. They live.

Humans are too obsessed with the body, and this obsession is big food for the mind. The mind is busy worrying about any issues with the body. Some worry about the appearance and how the body looks. And others worry about any *dis-ease* of the body. All this is uncommon in animals.

Everyone is striving towards perfection. If asked "Why are you so obsessed with your body, when it can take care of itself on its own?" most people will reply, "Of course we need to live better, we don't want to live like vegetables."

There is a difference between doing the needful and being obsessed.

Inner Self Integration improvises the concept of health in the mind, and this results in better health for sure. When you are happier, the body gains more vitality and immunity. And above all, you don't suffer even if the body has medical issues. In any case, for any medical condition, one will solicit medical intervention and the consequences cannot be guaranteed by the doctors. They just do the needful with their best capacity. So if you too do the needful for the body and live free from suffering, you live a complete life. Also, this way, the healing happens much faster. If you have an issue with your appearance or with that of others, with *Inner Self Integration*, you get liberated from the obsessions with the external looks of the body.

Q: If I am not concerned with my body, will I not put the body in danger?

A: If you live free from the clutches of the mind, you will live longer. You will be healthier and in no way putting the body in danger. Living without the obsession doesn't mean that you don't do the needful.

To elucidate this—if there is an injury in any part of the body, the body is an intelligent system that creates pain in that area and causes you to stop moving that area. The result is that the body's immune system gets into action. The cells start repairing the injured part. Of course, this is happening at the body level. If you have access to a medical doctor, you are supposed to consult and receive immediate first-aid, followed by treatment for healing.

But with the practice of this new way of living (which you will learn ahead), you will be able to perform all this action without getting too anxious or nervous. You will be as calm as selecting veggies at a salad counter. You don't ignore or neglect the body. Instead, you attend to the body calmly.

The *Inner Self* will be the judge and decide on what the needful is, at that very moment. If the *Inner Self* guides you to give the body rest, then you don't let your mind interfere with what is necessary. All of this is done in a systematic manner. Doing the needful and not interfering has to yield positive results. This is also being like nature.

Nature does everything perfectly and never interferes in the supposed-to- be-done. This body also is a masterpiece created by nature, and so is the mind. Only when you think you can interfere, misery begins. Doing the needful is not in your control. But watching the mind is. The moment you watch the mind, the mind is also supposed to come in its place on its own. Only when you have an obsessive attachment to the body through the mind, you create bondage, and then, you complicate the bodily process which would have happened in a simple manner.

Q: Everybody loves being healthy and in good shape. If I start practicing this way, will I not become careless about my health?

A: First, you complicate things and then, you look for solutions. This is alike the games of a child who is busy building and destroying sand castles at the sea shore. What is the need to pick up erratic eating habits and faulty lifestyles which lead to disturbed sleep regimens, and then look for solutions?

The right thing to do, in the first place, is to eat when hungry and eat the quantity that the body requires, in accordance to the physical work that you do. All animals do that. Even newborns do it that way. But you need to fulfil your taste buds, and when this gathers extra fat in the body, you need to run on a treadmill. Is this what you call being healthy?

Why do we have to disobey the amazing system called 'The Body' created by nature? What is the need to consume extra calories in the form of alcohol and partying late nights? The *Inner Self* guides you with all the wisdom. All you need to do is to connect, observe, and follow the guidance.

When you interfere, you are careless. When you follow effortlessly, you create health. In fact, health doesn't need to be created. It is the '*unhealth*' that you create by interfering. The absence of disease is health. *Dis-ease* to the body is created by your mind.

Q: Will my ailments and diseases go away if I connect to my *Inner Self* and start living a life free from the obsessive thinking of the mind?

A: When you are in a state of joy, the metabolism and healing mechanism of your body work more efficiently. It is very evident that thoughts impact the body. Psychosomatic disorders are great examples. These disorders are conditions where psychological stresses adversely affect physiological (somatic) functioning to the point of distress.

They can also result in dysfunction or structural damage to bodily organs through the inappropriate activation of the involuntary nervous system. In a state of rage, for example, the angry person's blood pressure is likely to be elevated, and his pulse and respiratory rate to be increased. When the anger passes, the heightened physiological processes usually subside.

Very often, people develop concern over the resulting physical signs and symptoms, but they deny (because of unawareness) that it is their emotions that have evoked the symptoms. Now, if negative emotions lead to a negative impact on the body, it is obvious that positive emotions will also lead to a positive impact on the body.

Hundreds of researches have been conducted on this topic. The only solution to a healthy life is to be joyful. To be in a state of joy is about not being worried. If you allow the mind to indulge in thinking, you allow the genesis of misery in the body as well.

Q: I want to live like a child. A child lives free of all thoughts of the body. How is it possible to live like that once again?

A: So true, a child that is two years old lives free of thoughts. He or she is made that way by nature. It is social learning that conditions the mind to worry. In fact, this is also a part of nature's action. We think we are doing it. Well, the answer is 'No.' Nature always does the just and the righteous. Nature made mankind evolve from monkeys—the mammals that were very curious to make new discoveries.

Humans are the only species that get bored. Do you know what boredom is? It is not accepting the present. Humans, in their attempt to create a solution to boredom, make new discoveries. So does a child, but what is different about the child is that a child doesn't continue thinking even when all the needs are met. Adult humans need more and more. You need a bigger car in a few years, a bigger house in a few more years, and in some cases, a different romantic partner. Isn't that funny?

A child plays with the same toys in the kindergarten; he or she plays on the same swings every day. The best part is that a child is equally happy every day with the same toys.

Have you ever thought of the reason? The same child is often bought new toys at home. But at school, he or she sees all other children playing with the same toys. So it is culture and harmony that play a major role. The object (toy) is not the objective. The objective is 'to play', of course, with the toy. But the highlight is in the playing, not on the toy. Even if the toy breaks, after a few minutes, they start playing with the broken toy itself. The best part is that even if they don't have the toy, they create their own imaginary game and start playing. They enjoy. The word 'En-joy' means being a part of joy.

CHAPTER
Twelve

Breaking the Cage of False Identity

This is a good position for you where you have understood 'the false.' The one who knows the false can go on the search to find the absolute – 'the true.' This false identity has been passed on from generations to the next. Eastern scriptures mention this false identity, they also mention the truth, the *'True Self'*, and the way to be in the absolute state that gives access to a free life, which is full of peace and joy.

This is the magnificence of truth, the moment you observe that there is an identity in the mind, it becomes false. The bigger question that arises is *'Is there someone who is observing this identity?'* It means that there is something more than this identity, and thereby, it is proven that the identity of the mind is not absolute. The next question that may arise in your mind is '*How do you see this identity of the mind?'*

This is simple, but you may go ahead only if you want to end your misery, only if you really want to go this route, and only if you want to believe in this process.

If the answer is *Yes*, then read the following steps and establish them in your mind. Your mind may reject the idea. It is normal if it does. You may still continue.

Do

1. Look at your whole life as if it is a running movie which, in any case, had to happen only in this design. You cannot change anything that has happened till now. If you could, you would.
2. Look at all the characters including yourself in the movie, as governed by the movie.
3. The movie is well-planned, and in all circumstances, it will go the way it has to. You need to think that even the thoughts that come to your mind came on their own. You are not the creator of these thoughts. Just be an observer seeing this character (your name) doing the acts, thinking, and feeling. Also, observe your mind. Even your mind is a component in the movie and will perform as per the design of the movie.

Don't

1. Don't believe the mind, even if it plants seeds of doubts. That is its job. There is duality in thinking, only because of the mind. The mind always wants to see things in two aspects – good and bad. This is a normal disease of the mind. The mind works like a rat.
2. Don't think that this method can be continuously applied. There will be times that you will get

caught in the trap of the identity again and become anxious about desires and life goals.

3. Don't think that your world will stop and you will stop functioning. You will, in any case, be doing your daily chores and fulfilling responsibilities. But you will do them with a free spirit and state of unaffectedness about the outcome. In simple words, not attached to the outcome.

Q: Indeed, I have felt many a time like this life has moved on in its own fashion as if I am in a boat that the river is taking away on its own. I often realise that I haven't done anything but this was all happening through me all this while. Is it actually true? But isn't this method going me make me feel like I am a loser, that I have no control over life? I want to live my life my way.

A: Yes, this is very much true. Start from the first day of your existence. Do you think you chose to be born of your own mother or father? Ask yourself—did you choose to be a boy or a girl? Or did you choose the colour of your skin? Now, if you didn't choose these basics and they happened on their own, so did all the other circumstances—like you choosing your stream of education, your career, or your partner (if you are married). All of it was merely a result of many coincidences.

Even if one incident—such as you changing your subject—changes, you would not be in your current career. Now go back a bit on this career trajectory, even the subject you chose happened because of a lot of reasons that were a part of the design. This is no race or match that you can lose or win. It is just a movie. Can you win or lose when you are watching a movie? You can just choose to see and not get obsessed. That is the only choice you have. The moment you choose to watch and forget the idea of winning or losing or controlling the movie, you are liberated.

In fact, you are always liberated. Only the mind is in bondage. The instant you adhere to this truth, everything in life will be just another scene for you, which in any case had to happen. If you could change, you would. Wouldn't you? And if you think you could, why didn't you? If you search for the answer to why you didn't, the previous answer will again reflect the design.

This has been always true and will always be true. Like the truth is always true. If not, it was never the truth. The success in watching a movie is to watch it. That's all. The moment you do that, you live a life of freedom, peace, and joy. That's the control over your peaceful existence. This is the game you need to win.

Q: **Just by seeing this life as if I am watching a movie, will I get out of the trap of negative feelings? Is it actually possible?**

A: Even reading all this in this book was a part of the design. Can you say that you chose to read it or that this is happening because all this was written in this book and it was beyond your awareness, a few days ago? Just like this is happening to you, everything is happening to you and around you. You are just an observer.

The instant you give your mind this task, you break the negative thinking pattern in your mind. Your mind is conditioned, rather, commanded to focus on or perceive the negative. Here, when you use this method, you force the mind to perceive the movie. This way, you get the mind into a different zone altogether. And then, it can't think and disturb you. If it is working right now at this moment, it can always work this way. All you need is practice.

Q: **When I applied this method, I felt the difference, but for a very short span of time. It felt different. But it didn't last long. Again the thoughts and doubts arise about whether this will work and if it is true? My mind is in doubt—it doubts when I see life as a movie, I am watching a forced reality. What should I do?**

A: It is normal for your mind to doubt. Imagine this is what the mind has believed for so many years now. And now, when a new way of life (which is exactly the opposite) is given to the mind all of a sudden, it rebels. This new way of *being* is centred on letting go of control to get peace, but your mind has been taught right from childhood that you need to do something to be at a better place. What a joke it is that you have been always chasing, and you could never reach that absolute place, could you?

You were made to be in the rut. Your folks, i.e., your parents, teachers, friends, and all those who mattered, and even those who didn't matter, have suggested and pushed you to do something in order to get somewhere. But have you ever seen them at peace with where they are? If so, follow what they say. Just stop and see, do they appear to live peacefully and do they truly exist in this world and operate from a peaceful position, a peaceful mind? The answer is NO. They have always advocated "to struggle." They themselves have struggled and in their hearts, are still struggling.

Only those who have really, effortlessly created will never say that they have created their life. You will find them saying that they have witnessed life taking shape on its own, and they will also mention that they played their role well without complaints. They are there. This is exactly something that you are learning in this *Inner Self Integrative*. If they followed this way of being, without even being aware that they followed it, you have also to do the same. And you have done it today. If it has worked for you for a few seconds, it means that it is true; and if truth has worked for you for a few seconds, it will work tomorrow, the day after, and ever after as well.

All you need is consistency. You need to consistently bring the mind back to this new reality. Yes, you may initially feel that the mind slipped back into the older pattern. This is normal. It is important to bring it back, whenever you can. The mind may be in that identity trap for longer durations. That's perfect. But you have to bring it back whenever you remember. Now don't make this bringing back a compulsive task and create a sense of failure in this as well. Do this practice very comfortably at your own pace. Feel good about being aware of all these game of the mind and access to the new reality. Don't measure the quality of doing the task; instead, feel good that you are on the track, the journey. You will certainly reach there. This too was a part of the design. And that will also happen if it has to happen.

Q: Sometimes, I really feel very low and lost. Is this method going to bring me out of those negative feelings?

A: Indeed, the whole objective of this *Inner Self Integration* is to bring you out of the misery, the negative thinking, and feeling. It is possible with practice. You will certainly live a great life where there is complete freedom from suffering in the mind. There will still be incidents happening around you, as designed for you. But you will be free—ever free. This is certain because you are free right now. This moment is also a part of the design. If you accept this as the actual reality in this very moment, your mind will be in acceptance of it, and you are free right now. After all, freedom is a concept of the mind, so is bondage. *Inner Self Integration* takes you beyond. Slowly, the book will attempt to bring you to that mode.

CHAPTER *Thirteen*

Acknowledging the Beyond

If you are not the identity, and if you are not the character in the movie as well, and all the characters and the movie are in the governance of the design, then who has made the design? Who is the creator of the design? And the biggest question—*Who am I then?*

Yes! The search for the answer to these questions is very critical.

Here is the truth. But a word of caution must be considered. The truth may appear very small, irrational, or even common. Very importantly, you need to follow the path that is told. To be a good student, you need to leave all your learning and knowledge behind. You can reach the truth or you can be your limited and myopic existence, i.e., the knowledge that you possess.

So either there will be the truth, which will liberate or there will be you— the false, the incomplete, and the limited you. Choose now. If you choose to follow the path and make a new discovery, allow your mind to receive and believe what is just going to be said.

THE FIRST TRUTH

You are 'THE SELF.'

The word *self* means 'individual' that is 'something that cannot be divided further.' The self *is* and the word '*self*' indicates something that exists on its own, because of its own self. The *self* can be simply understood as something on its own. The *self* is mentioned in eastern scriptures as *'Aatm'* also pronounced *'Aatma.'* This is a Sanskrit word that means 'on its own.'

Science, today, has been able to discover the smallest particle, that is the atom, is on its own, it is in motion, and exists on its own. Further researches talk about the sub-atomic particles that can be considered on their own.

Now very interestingly, if you look at anything—be it a plant, a stone, the sun, the earth, the moon—they are all individual, yet they are all interconnected, interdependent. The whole system is a composite one. The whole cosmos for that matter is running on its own. So can we say that there is a *self* in everything? The answer is *'Yes.'* You are the self. Let us experience this.

To know the truth you need to experience the truth, and only then, based on your own experience, you will be able to establish this reality in your system.

To do this, you need to follow the steps below:

Step 1. Sit down in a comfortable position, and don't move your body. Keep your eyes closed throughout.

Step 2. Now with eyes closed, see whatever you can. You see nothing, or darkness, or blankness. This is you. Here, there is no body, no mind, nobody, no situation—only you. You are simply existence. This is who you are. This is called the *self*.

Step 3. Slowly open your eyes. This whole world *is*. See your hands, this *is* the body, this body also *is*, and the situation *is*. All this keeps happening and is ongoing. It all changes, but you are not all this, you are the self, and this self always exists, you always are. Close your eyes again. Experience again that you are.

Step 4. Now slowly open your eyes and experience your existence with eyes open. Feel the calm and composure. You need to experience your existence with eyes open too.

THE SECOND TRUTH

The creator of the design is '*The Larger Self*.'

The *Larger Self* also focuses on the word '*Self* ' that means something that exists on its own, because of its own self. '*Larger Self*' is mentioned in eastern scriptures as '*Param Aatm*' which means 'the bigger arrangement that exists and operates on its own.'

Humans can also use the mind to discover the **Big Arrangement of Nature**—the game behind the games. Although it may not be seen, it is there. It is similar to how the air of the atmosphere covers the whole earth and you live in it, yet you are unaware that you are a part of it.

The cells in your body also have it. Like the sun's rays cover the earth and exist in the plants, the fruits, and the vegetables that you eat and thereby, are a part of your body.

Science refers to it as matter. It is also called Mother Nature, which implies the material world and its phenomena. The word *mother* is used because it is the creator. The creator of the design.

Scientists of all times have been struggling to analyse and understand the Big Arrangement of Nature, but they have not even been able to accomplish understanding 1% of all of nature. There is beyond—who knows. There are billions of coincidences behind the smallest event that happens at any point in time. Even the chair or the bed that you are sitting on is there because of a billion coincidences happening behind it. Your name is your name because of a billion coincidences that happened behind it. All this happens per the design that takes place in a moment, at a particular point in time.

Now consider the series of coincidences that make a scene in the movie happen. These coincidences occur in a flow, one leading to the other, that leading to the other, and so on. Even the shirt that you are wearing right now is an outcome of the flow of the series of coincidences. This is the design and the creator of the design. This design or the creator of the design is beyond the mind's purview of analysis and understanding. You need to believe it to experience it. Or you may intellectually begin to experience it to believe it. Both will lead to the same.

After all the awareness now, your mind will still have doubts. Your mind may ask, "*What is this I am reading?*", "*Many scriptures and books have mentioned this, but I don't believe,"* or even *"This is all imaginary."* It is normal for the mind to rebel—that's what it has always done. Only if you really focus on the outcome of believing this truth, you will have success. The false arrangement of things in this material world happen so fast that your mind will never be able to perceive the Science behind the action, similar to when you see the moving propeller of an aircraft, you barely see it because the aircraft is moving at such fast speed. Also, another metaphor could be associated with sunlight which has all seven colours blended in it so well, that you can barely see them.

Finally, acknowledging the beyond is the only solution to the misery and suffering. And this can be done by knowing the truth of the *Self* and *Larger Self.* Knowing can happen when you believe to experience or experience to believe the truth.

Q: If I am this *self*, why am I obsessed with the transient things that happen and pass. Why do I get affected?

A: This is the illusion that is created in the design. The design is based on the concept of change. Everything is changing every moment. The form changes with the movement of time. Isn't it obvious? The earth, which appears to be stationary, rotates at a speed of over 1400 km per hour. Indeed, everything that is at such a high speed of change appears to be stationary. This gives birth to the illusion that everything is real. When I say real, I mean solid and stationary.

When everything is changing, how is it real? It may be real one moment, but change the next. This means reality changes every moment. So what is reality, when it is changing? The only solution to this puzzle is 'to believe that very moment's reality and also remember that it will change.'

The state of unaffectedness can be derived in two ways—

The first is to believe that it all changes, so why bother.

The second way is to just make the mind focus a singular task – 'to observe.'

When the mind is busy observing every moment's reality the way it is at that moment, there is suffering. Suffering is because of the stagnation that the mind wants to create.

You get affected because you think you are the body, the name. You perceive the character and the scene as real. As a result, you feel the impact on you as if it is happening to you, although it is not happening to you. It is happening, but not to you—because you are the self and nothing ever happens to *you*.

Things may happen to the body and all the other characters in the movie, yet *you* always exist. If you follow the steps mentioned and also truly believe in the truth, you will not feel the impact. Just like nothing happens to the sky—the space where all the planets, stars, and so many celestial bodies exist—where so many reactions happen.

The universe is similar to a chemistry test tube in which so many experiments happen, and yet nothing ever happens to the air inside it and the glass test tube itself. Things happen and pass but the test tube stays, so does this universe – the illusion. And now on, for better understanding, nothing happens to the *self* and the *Larger Self*. Everything happens and vanishes in the *Larger Self*. Be with the truth, and you will start living free and in joy.

Q: Is this *Larger Self* really so powerful that it is running the whole world?

A: Not only the world, the whole universe is a manifestation of the *'Larger Self.'* The *Larger Self* is not only powerful, it is 'the power' itself. The power gets manifested in form of the world that you see. The world comes into existence because of this underplaying power. The power not only manifests itself in the creation of the objects and situations in the world, it also governs the continuous phenomenon of change. The *Larger Self* is the reason behind the matter of the changing universe. The beauty of this *Larger Self* is that it is all random.

A lot of easterners say that everything moves under the law of pre-written destiny. I wonder where it is written. I haven't seen it. But all I know is that the *Larger Self* works randomly. Everything that the eye can see and not see is governed by the *Larger Self* in form of the play of millions of coinciding incidents (which you call coincidences). These coincidences happen randomly, yet there is an order. So when it is all run by the *Larger Self*, why bother?

Q: If the is in control of things, am I also not a part of this *Larger Self*?

Then why does this *Larger Self* not take care of my problems?

A: Indeed your body is part of the *Larger Self*. The character is part of the play, the movie. But you are not the character. You are the *self*. You exist in the *Larger Self*. The way the *Real You* – '*the self*' exists on its own, for it is, in cause, similar to the *Larger Self*.

The character is created by the *Larger Self*. Isn't it? Who brought the body and this scene, i.e., the family and circumstances where this character is born? Of course, all this is caused by the *Larger Self* randomly. Therefore, the acts and role that are designed for this character are also well designed by the *Larger Self*.

It is your mind that creates the suffering for you by not wanting what the *Larger Self* has designed. Your mind rejects what the design has created. Your mind doesn't want the career, the boss, partner, and all other things that are perfectly designed by the *Larger Self.* This doesn't mean that the character will not act. All you need to do is to let the *Larger Self* create whatever design it creates in the movie and also let the character act. This is important to understand that you need to respect the *Larger Self* *'s* creation.

Also, that means that you need to respect the character's action because that is also not in your hands. If the character is acting, it is also the part of the design created by the *Larger Self.* You should not think that you have done anything. You are not the one to take claim for any achievements or even any losses. They are all a part of the design. Let everything be in motion the way it moves. And then, observe. You will create a great sense of joy. That state will be a state of pure freedom.

Q: What will I get if I believe the *Self* and the *Larger Self*?

A: Believe and then, you will get to know. How will you know whether you like the taste of a mango without eating it? The one who has never eaten a mango will be doubtful. But once eaten, the mango will become irresistible. That's what a mango does to almost everyone. Everyone likes the fragrance of the rose. But how does one explain the fragrance of a rose before actually smelling it?

PART *Three*

Rising Higher Into The True Self

If you have understood the truth of the true identity, you have to take your next step in the journey towards freedom from obsessive thinking and deprivation. You need to rise higher in the 'True Self.' Knowing the deeper aspects of your true nature—plain existence, you will be able to develop a sense of '*unimpactedness*.' Unimpactedness is ecstasy for those who have experienced it for a while. Most people confuse a heightened or excited emotional state as ecstasy. But it is not.

Unimpactedness is a state of emotional or religious frenzy or a trance-like state; originally, one involving an experience of mystic self-transcendence. Of course, there is nothing mystical about it. The fact that one has never experienced such calmness ever before makes it unique and mystical. Sometimes, some people do get it when there are sudden positive experiences—for example, when there is a sudden unexpected gift or accomplishment someday or when one gets a chance to meet a celebrity without notice. The feeling during such an event is ecstasy. It is possible to *be* in such a feeling by practicing the skill of being unaffected by any life situation that one faces. Of course, *Inner Self Integration* has a core benefit of establishing this state of unaffectedness. This will be taught further ahead in the book.

So being connected to the *Inner Self* facilitates this state of 'unimpactedness.' The more and more you practice

Inner Self Integration, the higher you grow in the self and the freer you feel from the challenges of life. This certainly doesn't mean that one denies responsibilities or ceases to grow materialistically. But one will be seen operating from a different paradigm.

Q: Will I become indifferent and insensitive to my people, this world, and my loved ones? I don't want to go into an unconscious state.

A: No, not at all. In fact, you will start loving your people more. With practice, you will even start feeling compassionate towards people who are not connected to you. However, that is at a later stage. When you become aware of your *Inner Self* – your true existence, you start becoming more sensitive to all that happens around you and all the people around you. This happens because the unnecessary thinking in the mind stops, and you get a chance to relish the experience of every moment of life. Hence, it is not a state of unconsciousness; rather, it is full consciousness of all the happenings.

Q: I want to live free and am interested to know more about my original *self.* Is it possible through *Inner Self Integration*?

A: Being aware of the *self* is not done with the intent of entertainment. It is an all-time, very basic, inquisitive need of humanity to know *the self.*

These basic questions occur to most people—"*Who am I?*", *"What am I living for?" and even "What is the purpose of existence?", "Why do we live?"* These questions come to mind only when one experiences meaninglessness in any pursuit that one is in.

The core reason behind these questions is unawareness of the truth. The unawareness of the *'self.'* When you get the answer by experiencing it personally, you begin to live free. This cannot happen by merely reading all this. The *True Self* needs to be experienced first and that too, on your own. You can never learn from the experiences of others.

With *Inner Self Integration,* you get a chance to experience *the self*, and when you know the *self*, you start loving life and living free in the true sense.

Q: Is it really possible to be unimpacted by all the situations of life?

A: Yes! With utmost faith and constant practice, you arrive at the state of 'unimpactedness.' The practice is very easy. One doesn't need to spend lots of time daily or do rigorous exercises or rituals to arrive at that state. The practice of *Inner Self Integration* is more about the sense that you build in your mind. Once you experience it for the first time, you carry it, and nurture it your mind with full dedication. There will be times that you forget and get into older patterns of obsessive thinking and materialistic entanglement. But then again, when you remember, you get back in the state.

The state of unimpactedness also needs to be understood correctly. It is not that you will have a strong body like steel or you will have no emotions. You will continue to live the same as you do now, but there will be no suffering. There will be emotions, but they will not continue for too long and make it difficult for you to operate. You will be seamless, free, and much more functional and comfortable in any situation while experiencing all the emotions. They will appear and go away like tides on the surface of the ocean.

Q: I have lots of dreams. I do want to achieve them but be unimpacted by the challenges that come my way. Is it possible?

A: It is normal for everyone to have dreams. If there is a mind, there will be thoughts. And if there are thoughts, there will be dreams. Dreams are like the seeds of the future. The future is created by these seeds. But the beauty of the larger dream "***The Larger Self*** is that it is the one who has created the mind and it is the one who has created the dreams in our minds. Not all seeds turn into trees. It is all a game of probability. It runs on its own randomly. Randomly, the dreams of yesterday and today turn into reality tomorrow.

The state of unimpactedness is a state where you will not be bothered by the seeds or the trees, yet acting comfortably. The character in the movie will perform his or her role very effortlessly as if he's perfected the art, but with the difference that he or she will not be attached anymore to the movie, the scene. You will not be bothered about the dream or the outcome of the performance, you will be cherishing the happening of the show, yet fully be there in the show.

CHAPTER *Fourteen*

End of the Misery, the Fear

Fears have always disturbed all human beings. No one can claim that they were never afraid in their lives. It is impossible because fear is a very natural and normal emotion. It is normal because that is how the nervous system, the body is constructed. It was created in all living species with an obvious objective of self-preservation and self-protection. Be it a snake, a lion, a monkey, or even a housefly, everybody has a response mechanism to threat and it is backed by fear.

Fear is the primal and prime emotion necessary for existence and survival. But the unique fact to be noted is that humans are not only afraid of immediate threats like other species, they are afraid of tomorrow. This is the only difference in the case of humans is that they have a mind that can think and that is like a sponge. It not only thinks on its own but also thinks depending on what other humans are thinking. This works like a chain reaction very spontaneously and very quickly.

Thoughts related to the emotion of fear spiral very fast. And then, the mind comes into action like a powerful, small, little motor that works on an auto mode, making a lot of humming noise. The mind needs a little clue or a cue about anything that can be a threat to ego, and it starts its work. This is supported by the central nervous system, which brings the body into its fight- or-flight response. In some cases, it even gets unconscious as a strategy to virtually run away from the scene, despite the body being there.

But the sad part—in the midst of all this play of the nervous system and the mind—is that you suffer. As long as fear is momentary and a response to an immediately threatening situation that you are able to deal with right then, it is okay. But if the fear is a pattern of the mind and you experience misery, then the need to work on it arises.

When you are aware of the *self*, the sense of fearlessness prevails throughout. You will have a new image of the *self*, the world, incidents, and people in the world. When you start operating from the *Inner Self*, you will be able to see the *Larger Self* and also the unity or oneness with the world. This liberates you from the pattern of the mind, and you witness the end of misery.

Q: I am always fearful about the future. I fear that something wrong will happen to me. Can I get out of this continuous fear in my mind?

A: When you have a sense of insecurity related to the future, you feel fearful. Insecurity means that you are not secure. This further means that something wrong may happen. There is an important inquiry that you need to make—"*To whom will the wrong happen?*" To the character in the movie or the *self*? There are a lot of things that keep happening in the *Larger Self*. In other words, incidents keep occurring in the world.

The only problem is that the mind keeps imagining and because of this, emotions keep forming. Fear is the imagination of a threat that may or may not happen in the future. These threats are not in anyone's control, and they are not a certainty. If they have to happen, they will.

Yet, there are two realities. First, that as of now, there is nothing wrong. Nothing is wrong or right. Everything is happening and just happening randomly. The whole universe is happening randomly. The human mind creates thoughts randomly. So why fear when it is all random? The second reality is that all that happens goes away. Nothing stays forever. Neither the World War nor the tsunami has stayed. Life goes on. People move in. This is the truth of the *Larger Self.*

So many things keep happening and going away, and all this happens randomly. The *self* is the true identity, not the body. The body comes into the world, and it goes away one day. All the scenes in between these two incidents keep happening randomly. Nothing happens to the *Real You – 'The Self.'* Relief only comes to those who are aware of the *Real Self.*

Q: How can I live free from fear, when everybody is so competitive and jealous, and there is so much wrongdoing all around?

A: What about all the competitive people who lived a hundred years ago? What about the competitive folks from a thousand years before that and earlier? All the competitiveness is in the mind. All the jealousy and competitiveness has to be paid for in the form of suffering. The wrongdoer suffers much more than the one to whom the wrong happens. The one who is wronged is wronged only once. Once the wrong is done and gone, the person is absolved from the fear. In simple terms, when the fear is known, it doesn't exist. Fear is always of the unknown, not of the known.

But for the wrongdoer, the emotions of fear persist forever; they grow with every wrong act. Fear is always of tomorrow, and when tomorrow comes in the form of today, the fear vanishes. The best part is that tomorrow will always be tomorrow. It is always unknown, and it unfolds on its own, so let it. The problem happens when the mind wants to interfere with the tomorrow. In some cases, when the mind wrongly analyses the past, the mind creates an imagination about the future.

This is the job of the untamed, undisciplined mind—to pass time. If you allow the mind to be idle, it will occupy its time cooking up imaginations of tomorrow with the ingredients of the past. The best is to give the mind the right task, an inquiry into the *self*, and a task to watch the movie that is running in the present. This way, the mind is busy watching the movie and experiencing the present. As a result, the mind can live free of this entertaining game of cooking up an imaginary future.

Inner Self Integration has a base of three principles which do away with the faulty imagination of the *Larger Self.*

Q: Can I become really bold and confident and live fearlessly with this new realisation?

A: This is the prime objective of the truth – to enlighten, which means take the darkness away. All the fear is insecurity. When there is security, there is no scope of fear. When you realise the truth, the mind doesn't remain undisciplined. It gets conditioned to follow reality. Consequently, there is only one emotion – the emotion of joy.

Q: I have always been a fearful child. How can all that conditioning go away?

A: As explained earlier, the mind can be conditioned. It has already gone through a series of conditioning. When you were a child, the older generation didn't know any other way of getting work done, except by using fear as the driving force. You were conditioned to be in fear of the consequences. The rule applied if you didn't eat your food properly, if you didn't study properly, or even if you didn't arrange your clothes properly. It worked perfectly.

How could they have thought of ways to do it differently, when their parents too used those very techniques? These techniques get passed down from generation to generation. Nobody explained the reward or the right logic behind doing the right thing. Explaining only one consequence has led to empowering this emotion—fear. The mind compartmentalised a consequence as 'good' or 'bad.' The truth is that 'A consequence is a consequence,' and the body and the mind respond according to the consequence. The consequence is the result of an event or a task done.

Nature or the *Larger Self* works on a simple principle of justice – the principle of cause and effect. The problem comes about when you term a cause 'good' or 'bad' because then you have to call the effect 'good' or 'bad.' Freedom can transpire when you know that nothing happens to the *self*, and nothing wrong ever happens in the *Larger Self.*

The *Larger Self* never falters. It always does right according to the cause. It is only a consequence of a cause. The inevitability of the effect according to the cause and *unimpactedness* of *the self* is liberating.

Being free can materialise only when the mind is made to focus on the truth. *Inner Self Integration* helps the mind focus.

CHAPTER *Fifteen*

Ending Shallow Desires by Stopping 'Thinking'

Almost all scriptures and religions recommend 'not to desire.' But has anyone spoken about the way to do it?

People often have this question—*"Is it practical to have no desires?"*

The answer is '*Yes.*'

All the frustration and suffering is undoubtedly because there is a mind, and the mind thinks. The mind either **wants** something or it **doesn't want** something. When the mind is not able to get what it wants, it suffers. Likewise, when the mind is not able to get away from something, it suffers.

So what is the way out? Is giving up desires the solution? No! No one can give up their desires. For that matter, as long as the mind exists, it has to desire. After all, the mind is also a part of the *Larger Self* as it is a part of the body. As long as the body exists, the mind too will exist. The mind is an auto play of thoughts, and thinking is desiring. Thinking centers on desiring the past, the present, or the future. It is classifying things as good or bad. Additionally, the senses provide input, which leads to thinking, which is followed by categorising the things, people or situations. This is a favourite pastime of the mind.

Not desiring is not possible, but not thinking certainly is. So if you learn to not think, the desiring will stop. But there is a flip side as well.

While doing so, many peoples' minds rebel and ask, *"Why should I not get what I desire?"*

Well, the answer is that, *"If there has been a thought, and thereby, a desire, the consequence has to be suffering."*

Metaphorically, if in winters, you desire summers, there will be heat and you will come to dread it one day. And then you desire winters, to finally dread that one day, as well. In fact, they had to happen in a cyclic fashion on their own. You have no control over it anyway.

Even to this, people argue, "I chose this profession, and I have a control over this fact." The truth in hindsight is that this profession has happened because of lots of causes, rather, millions of reasons that were at play. For example, parental inclination or support, teachers, the right colleagues, success, and so on. All reasons have coincidentally or randomly happened. They had to. For that matter, you had only this choice, so you chose. If you could choose something else, you would. You couldn't, so you didn't.

Even to this, you may argue, "I found this most appropriate for me, so I did choose." Even in this case, isn't that occurrence of the characteristic of the profession a reason beyond your control? So the choice is, in reality, no choice, but dependence on that characteristic. This is how the entire existence or the world happens on its own and runs on its own, including the character (the role) that you have been assigned in this movie.

When the mind accepts this reality and crystallises it, the thinking stops and thus, the desire ceases to emerge in the mind. The mind is too busy witnessing the play - *The Leela* of the *"Larger Self - The Larger I"*, that it doesn't think and doesn't desire. When it doesn't desire, it doesn't feel the suffering, and thereby, you will start living free.

Q: How can I have no expectations from anybody, from my own *self*, and from my life?

A: Of course, the expectations will arise. It is a normal phenomenon of nature. There will be action around you and inside your mind as well. However, you will not be a slave to the happening of the same particular thing. You will not be dependent on others who are doing a particular thing for you.

It is obvious if you pay your employee a salary, you expect them to work. Here, when you have realised the *Inner Self*, the *I* and the *Larger I*, it will be an obvious result that they need to produce, but for themselves. They will be choosing their consequence. You choose for yourself. You chose to be free and independent within your *'self.'*

To the outside world, you will be seen acting and performing, but within, you will not be feeling the stress and struggle of the outcome. If your role in the *Larger I* demands you to explain the relevance of the work to the employee, you will be seen doing it, but with a lot of compassion. This certainly doesn't mean that if despite communication, the employee doesn't perform, you continue paying his salary. You will then let him know that he has lost the job. The difference will be that you will have compassion for him even while letting him go.

Instead of anger or disgust, you will assume much more power and care for that employee, even while letting him go. You will know that you didn't do it and he didn't do it either, but only that it has happened. You will not have any anger or disgust, and not even happiness that he was asked to leave. Contrarily, you will be much more sensitive to him, and he will be aware that you are good, and that this has happened.

Q: Does being in a desireless state make me a saint? I don't want to be one.

A: It has been explained earlier that a saint is a holy person—someone who believes in the *Self* and the *Larger Self*. Being in a desireless state is like witnessing *The Leela,* conforming to its interplay, and just acting as part of *The Leela*, without adding and colours to the *self*. You will still be seen in action just the way you are now. The only thing that will change is the misery and suffering. You will not be suffering, and there will not be misery. Being a saint certainly doesn't mean that you will be leaving your house, your family, your hobbies, or your favourite food.

You will still continue living the same life. However, you will be much more open and conscious of life. Being with your friends and family will appear more satisfactory and having your favourite food will seem tastier. The only difference will be that you will no longer feel less when you are not able to meet your friends or family. You will not feel deprived and frustrated when you don't get your favourite food. The presence of your favourite dish will appear pleasant to you, and its absence will not frustrate you. This was explained earlier as the '*sukh*' or joy and happiness is in the true sense. The absence of suffering is referred to as '*adukha*' state by Buddha.

Q: How will I relate to all other people around me—my family, my friends, my colleagues— if I have no desires?

A: You will still continue living the same life; however, you will be much more '*there*' with your friends and family. The only difference will be that you will be in a state of much more joy. Your friends and family will be attracted to your permanent state of peace. They may start asking you to teach them the secret formula to being at peace all the time.

You will face challenging situations like anybody else, but you will take very little time to deal with the situation, compared to others. The right response to the situation will appear to you much quicker than to anyone else. As you will not be dependent on the future outcome, you will become seamless. And you will be able to acquire that by having no desires troubling you. This will happen when your mind doesn't indulge in thinking. With the practice of *Inner Self Integration*, your indulgence in thoughts will begin to decrease.

Q: I want to live peacefully. I don't want to live a boring life. Will a life with no desires and thoughts be boring?

A: As said earlier, life will not be boring; it will start appearing more pleasant to you. This is also called **Bliss**. Bliss will be explained in the coming chapters. Desires will arise in the mind like tides arise on the surface of the sea, to finally fade away. You live a coincidental life and live it randomly as it comes.

If there is a party and you see yourself as "the character" standing, dancing, and eating in the party, you will enjoy and relish the experience. If you are ill and lying in a hospital, experiencing pain in the body, it will not have any energy to bog you down or make you feel low. You will be in peace. This way, you have full control and the choice to live in peace. You live life witnessing and cherishing the complete experience of life.

CHAPTER *Sixteen*

*Sense of Completion Within **Self***

The *'I'* is complete within its own *Self*. That is why it is called the *Self*. The *Self* is something on its own. And when it is on its own, it has to be complete within its own self. Eastern scriptures say that the *'I'* is created by its own self and is caused for its own self, by its own self. It is the cause, and it is the purpose. In Science, the discovery of the universe is the cause and the effect itself. There are many examples of it.

The whole universe is a composite system, complete within its own self. The whole cosmos for that matter is running on its own. You are the *Self*, and you are similarly complete within your own *self*. When you practice *Inner Self Integration* or when the *Inner Self* is integrated into this life, you feel complete. This is something to be experienced. Only if one practices the technique, one can experience it. By merely reading and understanding at an intellectual level, it cannot be truly experienced.

When you experience the *'Inner Self,'* you will have no lack of anything, no aversion to anything, and there will be a sense of completion. You suddenly enter a realm where you experience unaffectedness from the daily hustle and bustle and the anxieties of life. Once you know it, you can never ever forget it, like you never forget swimming or bicycling. It's a knack. Once you have it, you have it forever. There will be times when some challenging situation sways you, but if you are integrated well, then again in some time, you will remember that you were free earlier. It may not occur to you immediately, but there will be a sense that it is possible.

It is just like health. If you have been overweight for a long time and suddenly, a technique works for you and you witness a magical reduction in your weight, you will remember it forever. You may not resort to that technique permanently and your weight may increase again, but whenever you cross the upper threshold, you know that the particular technique works for you. Then a day comes when you use the technique again.

Similarly, feeling complete is possible; and when you integrate to your *Inner Self*, it comes to reality. You suddenly feel no need for anything to make you happy and peaceful. However, even this is subject to change. A time may come when you forget, and the result is that you get back to getting obsessed with desires and accomplishments and start feeling anxious, frustrated, and low. However, the difference with having tasted the completeness for once is that even when you get off track, you will be aware that the mind is returning to the part pattern of thinking and desiring and feeling less. It then becomes very easy to start the practice again. The moral of the story is that **Practice Is The Key To Success**.

Q: Is it possible to not desire and yet feel complete?

A: It is the other way round. Not desiring will happen when you feel complete. To feel complete is an art.

When you feel complete, you will have no need for anything. Feeling complete is an emotional state. An emotional state leads to thoughts that are akin to it. When you are with a group of fun- loving people, you feel like having fun. When you are with people who are always criticising, in a few days, you start criticising. This happens because the mind is like a sponge. The pattern by which the mind absorbs patterns and learns is termed conditioning in Psychology.

The mind gets conditioned the way you want to condition it. If you don't condition it, it will voluntarily pick up negative conditioning. This is similar to the concept of health. Health has to be maintained on a continuous basis by providing the necessary nutrition and maintaining the necessary hygiene and by providing the necessary protection. If this is not done, the body becomes unhealthy without any effort. This is also explained in Science by the concept of *homeostasis.*

Homoeostasis is the property of a system in which variables are regulated so that internal conditions remain stable and relatively constant. So this way, the *Larger Self* and the *Self* and all the incidents and events are considered the perfect play of cause and effect to create the needed balance. Whatever the incident may be, it is aimed at the *Larger Self* to strike a balance. When you instruct the mind to witness this principle, the mind stops indulging in unnecessary thinking and desiring and thus, feels complete.

Q: If my mind wants something and I tell the mind that nothing is needed, is the mind not going to retaliate after some time?

A: Indeed, the mind rebels. But this happens to those who have not disciplined the mind. The mind has a unique characteristic—to think and imagine. Now, when you condition the mind to stop thinking, you are actually taking away the favourite toy or pastime of the mind. What will the mind do without the toy? It will get irritated and then, try to gain your attention by irritating you. There is a solution—don't take the toy away from the mind. Let it think. But instruct it to think the right thing.

When the mind is used for *self-enquiry*, it will be busy discovering the *Self* and the *Larger Self*. The mind will develop a habit of witnessing and cherishing the amusing acts of the *Larger Self*. It will begin to admire the little things and big things that happen in nature, the world. For example, the mind will even observe others' suffering when they are chasing a desire – big or small. It will get busy in drawing conclusions, judgements, and forming new beliefs. But this time, observation, judgement, and formation of beliefs will all be constructive and in the right direction.

This form of assessment and judgement will be liberating and facilitate fortification of the concept in the mind. There will be instances when it will observe its own self, and the moment it sees itself getting in the trap and the rut, it will get liberated. Similarly, sometimes it will go for the object of desire and later realise that it is pointless and did not get absolute satisfaction. *Inner Self Integration* doesn't captivate or limit the mind; it liberates the mind to see the truth. In the process, there will be needs and fulfilment of needs. There will be action and movement. The only difference being that you will not be bonded to the consequence or frustrated in the pursuit to create a particular consequence. You will be seen in action, by others, yet free from it.

Q: Why is it wrong to get what is needed and then feel complete? I feel complete and satisfied when I get what I want.

A: It is true that there is nothing wrong in getting what is needed, but what is the guarantee that there will be a sense of completion?

The sense of satisfaction is very limited and very momentary. The need to achieve the next target becomes even more compulsory in nature that the mind takes you back to the rut of the fulfilment of desires.

Here, whatever naturally comes your way and whatever action happens naturally, you allow it to happen. There is a subtle difference here.

You need to note that you are allowing the action to happen and not allowing the mind to think that you are the doer of the action. The action happens; you don't do it. You just become a part of the happening of the action. This is the only way to achieve the purest and most absolute satisfaction. The other route, of course, is to be a go-getter. In this route, there is no permanence in the satisfaction achieved through the action. Certainly, once success is achieved by acting towards getting the desired object or situation, it adds to the notion that you have done it. This gives food to the mind—a belief that everything is in control and that anything can be achieved. This, in other words, can be understood as 'ego.'

However, success will not be achieved every time. There are so many millions and billions of probabilities for the consequences of action other than the expected. When the desired consequence doesn't happen, there will be suffering and misery. This doesn't mean that the action should be stopped. No one will ask you to stop performing the action, in fact, you cannot stop the action. The only fact to note is that if you operate from the ego, you are bound to suffer.

The ego is the false concept of identity that is not inclusive but exclusive in nature. It talks only about the character in the movie. Whereas the truth is that the character exists because of the movie, the character exists because so many other things also exist, other characters, the stage exists. But who is running the whole show—only the character? Or the director? Or the script writer? The best and only way to absolute satisfaction is seeing the character performing the role and the scenes happening to the character and the character performing in the scenes.

Q: Isn't feeling complete a sign of weakness or surrender?

A: You do not need to surrender. You need to learn to unite with the ultimate, the most powerful, rather the only power that is behind the play, behind *The Leela*. It is the *Larger Self - The Larger I.* When you integrate the *Self* to the *Larger Self*, there is a question of losing. And no question of winning either. Winning or losing against whom?

It's like there is a government, and you are the king. The government operates through the king, and the king operates because he has his government. It is similar to the concept of the king and kingship. The king *is* because he has the kingship and the kingship exists through the king. The king needs nothing and fears nothing. This is so because whatever is right for the king is supplied to him, in any case. The true king doesn't need to ask or desire.

CHAPTER *Seventeen*

Rejoicing in the Unacknowledged Blessing

Deprivation is one way of living. This kind of living is living like a beggar. The undisciplined mind will always ensure that you live like a beggar. The mind will always look at the other, compare, and find out what it is that the other has and you don't. Even if you are a king, if your mind is undisciplined or unaware, it may even look at a beggar who is young, hearty, and healthy and make you feel less. This is true for everyone who is not aware and not liberated.

The solution is only one—connectedness to the infinite abundance. This has been mentioned by a lot of self-help gurus as a passing reference, information. But it is more important to practically be able to do it. You are the *self*, and you are similarly so complete within your own *self*. With the practice of *Inner Self Integration* and with the integration of the *Inner Self* in this life, you feel connected to the *Larger Self* as well. And then, you attain an awareness of the beyond. You realise that the character in the movie has been provided perfectly with everything that it needs. There is nothing the character is short of, ever.

The mind looks at other characters and other's movies and picks out only one part to compare with. However, if you see their complete movie, you would never choose their character. You will like their movie far better, only for the reason that you have not seen their movie completely.

You just see one perk that is awarded to them in their movie. The law of cause and effect based on which the *Larger Self* operates in everyone's movie and in everyone's world. Your world appears as incomplete to you as their world appears to them.

The situation that is best is when someone you compare yourself with actually lives in a state of completeness and abundance. Some people have it in them naturally and some don't. You need to connect, and then, you will realise the abundance that you are surrounded with. This is something to be experienced. Only with the practice of the technique, one can experience it. Otherwise, by just reading and understanding at an intellectual level, it cannot truly be experienced.

When you experience the *Inner Self*, you will not be deprived of anything, there will be no aversion to anything, and there will be a sense of completion. You have always been provided with everything that you need, and you will always be provided with the blessing. The only trouble with you is that you don't acknowledge it. How can you, when you can't see it. You are not able to see it because your mind isn't free to see it.

It is busy looking for deprivation, like a painter who paints a picture never finds the picture complete. His eye is always identifying imperfections. This is the ill of being a creator. Only the creator knows that there is something more that could have been done. This is the mind's hobby. The mind looks at deprivation which leads to a feeling of aversion, despair, and thereby, misery.

The way out is by connecting to the *Inner Self.* That is when you will get a chance to see the wholesomeness and abundance that the character is blessed with. The word 'blessing' means to confer prosperity. The movie always confers the character the prosperity it requires.

Q: I see myself as being incomplete and less. How can I tell myself that I am blessed when I am not happy with my life?

A: It's the other way round actually. Only if you are happy, will you be able to see that you are blessed. This can happen only when you when you are aware that the Real You is complete. With the whole concept of integrating the *Inner Self* with this life, you will be able to see that you are complete.

The sense of completeness will liberate you from the feeling of less. This awareness cannot be intellectually understood. You need to practice *Inner Self Integration* to experience it. Only when it is experienced, the mind will be able to remember it. It will permanently be etched in its memory that the *'I'* is complete.

Q: If I see myself as blessed already, what is the need to wake up every day and work? Will the *Larger Self* not provide me with everything?

A: Most people who are introduced to the truth for the first time have the same question. When you know the hidden truth that governs the whole world around you, you will see that like everyone else, even the character that you play is in action. You have always and will always be playing your role. *The Larger Self* will get that done from you. So the action will be carried out as long as the body is alive. *The Larger Self* provides you with all that is needed and will ensure that you do whatever others need.

Q: What happens to those who are really needy? Doesn't the *Larger Self* see their misery? Why does the *Larger Self* not provide for them? What are they suffering?

A: Why do you worry about others? You need to sort out yourself first. Only when you are yourself liberated, you can think of others. Are you liberated yourself ? Have you understood that the movie is complete for you and you are blessed with all that you need? Have you understood that the movie expects your action towards the role that is assigned to you? Who knows you had a critical role to play in the movie of the deprived? What do you know about their movie? It is easy to comment from a distance. All you need to do is simply pass a statement.

The purpose of human existence is to realise the truth. When their time comes, they will also realise the truth. There are people amongst them who realise and create the truth. There is no need to sympathise, however you must empathise.

Only when you get to know their deeper story, you will realise that the challenge is equal for the other. Suffering is based on the perception and judgement of experience. How they perceive and judge their experience is up to them. Even realising the truth doesn't happen to everybody. You are on this journey and reading this book because you have to see this scene in the movie because it has occurred randomly for you here.

Similarly, their scene also appears in front of them. The purpose of realisation of the truth is to come in agreement with the *Larger Self* and have a sense of oneness with the actions performed by the *Larger Self*. The moment this is done, the idea or the thought of righteous action occurs to the mind and steps are taken towards that path and the scene changes. Only the solution to any problem brings the difference to the situation, merely feeling miserable will not help the situation.

There is a solution to every misery. And that is—creating peace within. Peace within can be created by connecting to the *Inner Self*. Do it and then talk about it. All you must do is to go to the fellow miserable human you know and empower him by teaching him the truth and enabling him to see the solution (to his problem) arising in the *self*. That is better than talking.

Q: If life has really provided every character with all that is needed, why is there suffering?

A: Suffering is due to stagnation. The mind is stagnated in the particular event in the particular point in time. It doesn't want to move. The whole world and the cosmos are in movement, but the mind wants to change the phenomenon. The mind wants to stay in the past and suffers because of that. The mind wants to see the old days at school, wants to see the photographs and feel sad. No animal does that and no plant does that either. Nature believes in motion and just flows with the time.

The mind, like a small child, doesn't want to believe that the toy has served its shelf life and is gone now. The child cries when the toy doesn't work. So does the mind. In fact, when you grow up, it becomes even worse. That's when the memory comes in. When the child has cried enough, maybe for half-an-hour, he or she forgets about the toy forever. This happens because the normal pattern of the mind of the child is similar to that of an animal that has lost a limb. The animal cries for a while and then forgets. The animal and the child do not cry again comparing the past with the present. But when you grow up and the memory becomes more profound, you go back in the past and start feeling miserable.

Memory is a characteristic of the brain and the mind that can't be taken out of the system. However, there is a solution. Once you have experienced peace in the midst of a challenging or unpleasant or undesired situation, you can use the same memory to remember that peace is possible. You can use the memory to find out what your *Real Self* is and what the world is, in reality. You can choose to remember that you are not the character. The character has appeared in the world to go away one day, so why all the fuss.

You also need to know the reality behind this world. You must remember that this world is a random play of the *Larger Self* that has billions of characters and situations to create the existence of any incident or one person in front of you today. Don't you see it as a mystical and magical creation? Go back and try to remember one new person that you met today, or yesterday, or the day before. Have you thought that there are multiple reasons that only that person has appeared in front of you? All the scenes of the movie randomly and continuously come into existence, every moment, on their own, and in the best form for you. All you need to do is to see the blessing in the scene. Only practice of connecting to the *Inner Self* will make this happen for you.

PART *Four*

The Supreme Reality 'I'

If you look at the life that you have lived till now, you will see that everything happened in a set fashion. There were thousands of scenes that appeared in the movie—some appeared pleasant to the mind, some unpleasant, some created confusion and ambiguity, some created anger, some created sadness and despair, some surprise, and so on. But one truth always prevailed - the "*I*." There was this "*I*" that was always there and observed all these scenes. This "*I*" experienced all the emotions all this while. At the same time, "*I*" was there as it is. Nothing ever happened to the "*I*." "*I*" watched all the scenes happening in the movie and went away.

The scenes were like the play of astronomical events that happen in space. Space always remains intact—there are cosmic explosions, transitions, and formation of stars and fading of the stars, but space always remains as it is. It can also be compared to the earth. There are so many changes that keep happening on the surface of the earth, but the earth is always the earth. Humans create buildings on earth, floods happen, earthquakes, riots, and natural calamities happen, but the surface of the earth is always there intact, unaffected. The best part is that this has been happening for millions of years, maybe more, who knows! But the truth is earth, the truth is the space—the truth is the "*I*." "*I*" has always been there.

To experience it, consider this example—just look at your hands. These hands were never there in this world once upon a time, then there existed small baby hands, and then, they grew bigger and bigger, and now, they are there in this shape and form. Ask yourself, "Who watched the form and size of the hands change all these years?" The "*I*" has always been the same. It is you the true nature, the supreme reality. You exist from within the body. You are the body, yet not the body. You were always there in the same way—the reality—the "*I*."

This "*I*" can't be described in form. This "*I*" was always formlessly giving form to the world that exists around it. Here, you need to understand what "Giving form to the world around" means. Now look around at the clothes the body is wearing now and look at the objects around you. Through some or the other manner, you are responsible for all these things around you. You are the reason for these things—the world around you.

Right now, your mind may say that you have not created some things, but the truth is you are allowing those things voluntarily or involuntarily, which gives the world a form the way it is in front as of now. This way, "*I*" is the supreme reality that exists in everything. It has directly or indirectly created the world as appears to you, around you, for you. The word 'Supreme' denotes the power, the *onlyness* responsible, the only creator. Of course, there are other "*I*" also around. And there is the interplay of all the "*I*." That interplay is the "Larger I."

CHAPTER *Eighteen*

The Ever Free 'I'

There is no bondage to the "*I*." "*I*" is always free from all the happenings, incidents, events outside in the world. The impact of the events happens only when the mind is allowed to perceive in its own free way. The mind has the habit of perceiving anything as good or bad. That is why people experience suffering. But above all, there is the "*I*" where nothing ever happens. This "*I*" needs to be experienced first, and then, the mind can witness freedom. There is no compulsion to believe all that the mind says or does.

Of course, the mind needs to be disciplined and trained. It need not be controlled or suppressed. But with continuous practice, it gets disciplined. There will be instances where the mind will still get stuck with its objects of desire. It will get into the process of cyclic thinking. All you need to do is watch the mind doing so. The moment you begin watching the mind, you will know that it is a useless action resulting from the past conditioning of the mind.

Now when you watch the mind, something new will happen. You will not be flowing with the mind, in fact, you will be able to see the mind as if you are sitting at the bank and seeing the river flow. You may get irritated with the river, but this time, you will not drown in the river. The difference will be that in a few minutes or a few hours, you will discover a break in the continuity of the thought cycle.

This new discovery will make you experience the free *"I."* The *"I"* has been free always. But as the *"I"* did not know it, the mind had control over everything. For example, there is a sleeping lion hidden inside the forest. Monkeys are creating a mess all around in the forest. Only when the lion is awake and the monkeys are aware of this, they climb up the trees and become silent. Although the inherent characteristic of the monkey remains, the monkeys will always be aware that the lion exists and not create much drama. Of course, something they will always keep doing and the lion is aware of, is that they exist without impacting the forest much. So this *"I"* was, is, and will always be there. Earlier it was not a known entity, now with the practice, it is not.

So if you are with the true, with the free, there is freedom. The character or the role will still have to be played but with freedom—freedom from anxieties, deprivation, frustration, fear, anger, etc.

Q: With the chores and responsibilities of daily life, how can freedom be continuously exercised?

A: You need to operate from the sense of the *"I"*—the free *"I."* That's all. All this while, you have lived life believing that it's true and it's happening in reality, giving high importance to events and expectations, when the truth was something else. No desire can be completely fulfilled. After every desire is fulfilled, a new object of desire will trigger the mind, and the chase will begin all over again. Is this a life of freedom? Every day you wake up thinking that there is a need for a new shirt, new watch, a new car, a new work goal. You keep chasing these goals, and one day, life comes to an end.

There are very few people who don't take these goals too seriously, yet you find that they achieve these goals more than you are and achieve many more things than you. If they are comfortable in their roles and life, they don't need to understand all these concepts of *self*. They somehow have that knack, and they may not even know it. There is no need to know it. There are also some people who can't bring themselves to believe the concept of *self*. There is a nice proverb in the Arabic language that explains this well:

He who knows not and knows not that he knows not is a fool; avoid him. He who knows not and knows that he knows not is a student; teach him. He who knows and knows not that he knows is asleep; wake him.

He who knows and knows that he knows is a wise man; follow him.

If you belong to the second or the third category, the concept of *self* will liberate you, otherwise, it will not.

By awakening yourself to the spiritual realm of the *Inner Self*, you will experience and cherish freedom in such a way that you will never get caught in the trap of the mind for long periods at a stretch. Thereafter, you will perform your chores and responsibilities with a lot more intrinsic happiness and freedom.

Q: **Once when start this practice, will the mind never disturb me again?**

A: Of course not. The mind will not have much power to disturb you, but it will not be dead. The mind is the only consciousness that humans have in contrast to animals, plants, and the non-living. Here with *Inner Self Integration*, we are integrating you, your life, and your mind with the *Inner Self*, which is power itself – the ultimate. This integration is only done using the mind. After all, the mind is the medium to realise the *Self* and the *Larger Self*. The mind is a tool that can help us understand and perceive. When the mind perceives things in the right way, life appears very simple and effortless.

Q: **People in my life don't do as much for me as I do for them. Will I be dealing with the issues that I face at work and in my personal relationships?**

A: Do you do things for them without expectations, or do you expect some good for yourself when you are doing things for them? This has always happened and will continue to happen until you understand the game of the mind. If you feel they are not doing as much as you do, doesn't this arise out of an expectation? You do and you expect in return. This is the game of the mind.

Your mind brings others into the game, and when others don't respond the way the mind wants them to, you experience suffering. When your mind sees this, it makes you react to them and finally, there is no gain. This doesn't mean one should stop doing things for others. In any case, this couldn't have happened any other way because this is how it was randomly created by the *Larger Self* at that very point in time.

Now there are two steps to deal with the situation. First, see all the thoughts (in the mind) and actions of the character as a play of the *Larger Self*. And then operate from the *Inner Self*, where there is no 'doing' happening. With the *Inner Self*, you exist effortlessly and exist freely. Being integrated with the *Inner Self*, you will be able to see that there is a character and there is a mind and that both are in action.

At that paradigm, all expectations vanish. Action will still happen, but it will be the right responsive action that will have an abundance of harmony, balance, and affection towards everyone around you. You will be seen harmoniously functional in the world around and at the same time, in a state of unaffectedness. You will be able to love the lead character and all the others in the movie. Whenever the lead character has a need, he or she will be able to very humbly share his or her rational needs with the other characters in the movie. Some will respond more than expected, some exactly as expected, some less, and some none. But in the end, all will appear equal in value to you.

Q: Freedom from thinking cannot free us from action. The world will still exist, and there will be days when we need to be strong to deal with tough situations. Isn't that true?

A: There is nothing true in the long run. Billions of people were born and died living this rut. There have been generations of people on earth who have gone by living this game of actions and reactions. You can't get away from it. Characters exist, as does this movie. All you need to remember is that you are not the character, and you are not the movie. Nothing ever happens to the Real You.

If you remember this, you will see the character performing the most appropriate action in response to the situation. This may be attributed to the fact that the situation will simply appear as a situation to you and not as a tough situation. This will make the mind comfortable and allow it to connect to the self who has the infinite wisdom (or potential) to deal with everything.

This is similar to how a really good plumber very effortlessly sees the water circuit and comfortably observes the blockage in the circuit and identifies the point where the water is stuck. If you observe him carefully, he is very calm throughout. If you ask him, he has just one reality in his system, that water is there, and its core characteristic to flow. All he needs to have is a calm mind, only then he can look into the circuit in an organised manner and observe the flow of the water at every consecutive point. He is aware of the reality that water is present and will flow.

The only fundamental that he remembers is cause and effect. There is a cause that leads to an equal effect. Similarly, you need to know that everything passes and all changes and all happens randomly and is a creation of the *Larger Self*. You also need to know you are not the cause and not the effect either. By integrating with your *Inner Self*, you live free yet all you do the actions, which leads to more fruitful results. But again, intellectual understanding of the *self* alone doesn't work, one needs to experience by practicing.

CHAPTER *Nineteen*

Bliss Unlimited

The *Larger Self* is the cause of all existence that can be seen by the eyes. It is a random play that is perfectly designed at every moment and in evolution, at every point. Everything is governed by this phenomenon. The word 'perfect' must not be misunderstood. Perfect is neither good nor bad. It is the perfect consequence of some cause. The cause and effect are the *Larger Self* itself. When the *Larger Self* creates something every moment, it also creates a complete object and a complete situation.

It is only the mind that sees the situation in isolation and from the point of view of deprivation. The mind is an intelligent system that can create anything. It can create abundance, and it can create deprivation in the same situation just as easily. It perceives the event or situation with an objective of looking at it with a particular focus, with a particular objective. And it is so sharp that it can prove either hypothesis. This is similar to the metaphor of the 'glass of water.' It is the mind that can prove that the glass is half-empty, and it is the same mind that can prove that there is water in the glass.

When you connect to the *Inner Self* and become aware of the fundamental truth, you get a chance to realise that the *Larger Self* does the arrangement perfectly for everyone. Although the perfectness cannot be seen with the mind's old pattern of perception. The mind's natural pattern of perception is to find imperfections and see less. This pattern of the mind is natural too because the mind is governed by the primitive instincts of survival.

In contrast to these primal instincts, one can choose to live a life free of the mundane need to survive. All that needs to be done is to make the mind work towards the truth. This is the ultimate purpose of human existence—to realise the *Self*, realise the *Larger Self*, and the truth.

Everyone is so blessed right from birth until the body ceases to exist.

CHAPTER *Twenty*

'I' In the Larger 'I'

The 'I' is part of the 'Larger I.' This needs to be understood properly.

Using the metaphor of the body will work.

If someone asked you, "Where is the body?" your immediate response will be to point out to any part of the body and say, "This is the body." You may point at the hand or the chest and say, "This is the body."

When you point at the hand or the chest as the body and then ask yourself "Is the hand the body?" The answer may be, "Yes, the hand is the body."

If the hand is separated from the body then it no more remains the body and only then it becomes something separate from the body. But as long it is connected as one united part, it is the body. Similarly, the "I" exists in the "larger I." The "I" is not a part of the "Larger I." It is the "Larger I" manifested in "I."

Another example can be of the mountain. A mountain is the earth, and the earth is the mountain. If someone had to see a mountain from the moon, he would refer to it as earth because it is in the earth. Similarly, a finger is the hand, and the hand is the finger too. The hand performs a task through the finger, and the finger exists in movement and life because of the hand. The same way the "*I* or the *Self*" exists in the "*Larger I* or *Larger Self*" and they function as one.

The only difference is that there is no direct expression of the "*Larger I*"—it just expresses itself in numerous forms. It appears in forms of magical mystical expressions. Who is moving the earth around the sun? What makes the sun burn and shine brightly to give light? What makes a seed turn into a tree? And what makes the soil nurture the seed and turns into a sapling? What makes the seed appear on the tree in first place? Isn't all this enough to understand the magic or in simple words, the expression of the *Larger I*?

The "*I*" is also so free and has the "*Larger I*" in it. The seed has the tree in it, and the tree has many seeds in it. The "*I*" has the "*Larger I*" in it, and the "*Larger I*" has many "*I*'s" in it. All that you need to understand is the existence of the "*I*", that is also called "*Inner Self*." In the subsequent chapters of the book, you will learn the way to connect to the "*Inner Self*." This needs to be experienced. And then, with experience, you will be ready to experience the manifestation of the "*Larger Self*"– "*The Larger I*."

When you go to the *Inner Self*, the ability to create will become clearly visible to you. You will realise that the *Inner Self* has created the entire world that is visible to your eyes. Every single thing has been a result of the thoughts that came about in the *Inner Self*. The *Inner Self* has empowered the mind to take action. That has resulted in the occurrence of things, situations, and people—the world where your body (the character in the movie) exists.

So for example, you are reading this book because the *Inner Self* empowered the mind to buy the book or pick up the book and continue reading, right up to this page. Every incident is a manifestation of the "*Larger I*" through the "*I*."

Ask yourself, "Where did the thought to read this book come from?" How is it all happening?

Indeed, everything is happening randomly by the interplay of the "*Larger I*."

PART *Five*

Overcoming Pain in Relationships

CHAPTER
Twenty One
Spiritual Belonging

This is a journey towards creating happiness and love in your relationship. It is natural for your mind to be curious to know how to make your relationship better, how to resolve issues, and how to create a love-filled relationship. There are chances that your mind will begin to doubt if the problem can be solved. Strangely, it is the mind itself that wants to resolve the issues, and it is the mind that doubts. But the truth is that the problem can be solved only through this mind.

Many a time, the mind believes that problems are big and they cannot be solved. The mind usually looks at some external reason or the other person as the source of the problem. It reasons that if these external reasons go away or your partner makes personal improvements, your relationship will become good. Most people think the same way. However, nobody has ever benefitted by sitting on the shore. You have to act on your life and make it better.

So let us start this new journey and turn it all around. For this, the first thing that you need to know is 'Love.' Most people think love is a feeling that exists for someone or between two people. Indeed, it is an intangible feeling, so ambiguity around it is very obvious.

Psychology as a Science defines 'love' as a variety of 'different feelings', 'states', 'attitudes', that range from interpersonal affection (like "I love my mother") to pleasure (like "I loved that meal"). Love is also defined as an emotion of 'strong attraction' and 'personal attachment.' It is also seen as a virtue that represents human kindness, compassion, and affection. This form of love is not only expressed towards other humans, but also to one's Self or animals, nature, or anything. You may or may not understand all this so easily. But if you knew a much simpler meaning of love, it would be easier for you.

Q: What Is Love In the True Sense?

A: Love in the true sense is "an unselfish act, done to ensure the good of the other."

I repeat "Love in the true sense is an unselfish act, done to ensure the good of the other."

This needs to be understood well.

The first word used here is **'unselfish.'** 'Unselfish' means 'not centred around the self.'

The next word in the statement is **'act done'**, which means that one needs to consciously do something that involves 'wilful effort.' This act needs to be done **effortlessly**.

Only then it can be called love. The last but most important part of the statement is '**done to ensure the good of the other**.'

Now, who is going to decide 'what is good for the other'? 'The other' of course. Everybody wants to be loved the way they expect. This is a very common problem amongst couples. Very few people know that 'love' is perceived as 'love' only by the eyes of the one who is loved. When you love your partner your way, it is like you are gambling. You may win or you may not. Nobody knows whether your effort is worth it or not. Who knows, your partner wanted you to put in half of the effort, but because you love more, it becomes a put-off for your partner. Maybe your partner wanted something else, and this is why your partner snaps at you for your effort.

Q: What is Marriage?

A: Marriage is The Union of a Man and a Woman as Husband and Wife.

The first word in this definition is '**union**' which means one. Only when they become one, they can be called a united team. In some relationships, the couples become united much before the wedding. But in most cases, couples do not unite, even many years after the day of the wedding.

The statement *"Marriage is The Union Of A Man And A Woman As Husband And Wife"* is wonderful as it mentions the words 'man' and 'woman.' This highlights their being different. How they accept each other's differentness marks the success of the marriage. The words 'husband' and 'wife' refer to the roles that they expect each other to play. The two have to unite and play their respective roles, as expected by each other.

Now that you know the definition of "love" in the true sense and "marriage", you need to become capable of loving in the true sense.

For this, you need to inculcate the following components in your personality—integrity, a sense of belonging, total ownership, being there for each other, loving, seeing through, asking, and receiving.

Q: How does one have integrity in a relationship?

A: Integrity is a personal choice to uphold oneself with consistency. If you intend to have a happy relationship and intend to create a functional marriage, you need to make a personal choice to love your partner, regardless of all else. Your mind may have obsessions or negative judgements about your partner that may be based on some negative experiences. But if you have integrity, you need to shut your mind and remain committed to consistently loving your partner. This is the first premise of loving truly.

It is rightly said that "*Your partner is the mirror to your personality.*" This means that if your partner reacts badly, then maybe at some level, you do not exercise your integrity towards your partner. Your mind may rebel as of now, but it is true. Of course, seeing one's own self in a state of loss of integrity is not easy. But it is possible that you do not operate from the position of integrity. Those who have integrity will listen to their partner and find out what is disturbing their partner.

The following chapters in the book will help you gain all the skills necessary for this. But it is your responsibility, towards your own self, to have the integrity to love your partner, 'the way he or she wants to be loved.'

Q: How does one create a sense of belonging?

A: A sense of belonging is another critical factor that makes a marriage successful. In fact, a sense of belonging is a must for any relationship— be it your work, your family, or any relationship. The word 'belong' comes from the word 'along.' 'Along' means 'to be with'. Therefore, belonging implies 'to be with.'

If you are sincere with your partner, he or she will sense it. You need to be with your partner emotionally, psychologically, logistically, financially, and practically, in all ways that you can, and also in all ways that your partner thinks that you can.

At this, your mind may rebel and say, "My partner has unrealistic expectations." If all this while, you have been with your partner in all other areas except for one, you can ask for help for that particular area.

Also, there may be a few things that your partner expected from you but he or she never shared them with you. That is probably why the situation has turned adverse now. For a few moments think, 'What are the things your partner is expecting from you?' And in which situations were you not there with your partner?

Q: How does one take ownership in a relationship?

A: The word 'ownership' means 'to own.' Owning your partner is about being a guardian to your partner. Your partner is your family now. You have been living as a brother, a sister, a daughter, a son, and so on. But now, you have to play a role of the guardian of this new family, that is, your partner and you. If you do not establish this ownership in your own self, your partner will surely sense it. This is the reason for conflicts in a relationship.

As an individual, everyone lives an independent life, but when you own your partner, you are always supposed to think in the best interest of your partner. Your parents have always done the same for you. They always had the sense of ownership for you. Another example that you can take is of your career. If you are successful in your career today, it is only because you have taken ownership for your career and your organisation all this while. Similarly, you need to take ownership for your partner and your relationship. And as a result, very soon a day will come when your partner will also have a sense of ownership for the relationship.

Q: How Can You Be There for Someone?

A: Who would want to buy a shoe that does not come with the guarantee that it will last long? Are relationships not much more serious compared to a shoe? So if one cannot even buy a shoe that does not last, how can one accept a relationship that does not last? Everyone needs a guarantee that he or she will be loved forever. It is a very basic need, even for animals.

A baby cub becomes anxious when it is not able to spot its mother. An elephant cries when it is parted from its partner. Similarly, all humans want to be loved forever. You need to assure your partner that you will be there forever. This gets registered in your partner's conscious and subconscious awareness. When you make this commitment to your own self, it can be said that you have the right concept of love.

Q: What is the way to love?

A: Being in love is different from *loving*. If 'love' is a noun, 'loving' is a verb. It is about actively doing things for the partner the way he or she expects. You need to be proactive in expressing this gesture of *loving*. The real test of love is at the time your partner is not able to love you back, but you continue to love proactively. Your mind may doubt that this is 'giving in' or 'sacrificing.' No! It is not. This is *loving*.

You either love or you don't. And if you love, you always *love* your partner, regardless of anything. The best evidence of *loving* can be seen in nature. All of nature ensures that it loves all the life forms, at all times, just like a mother loves her child, irrespective of anything. All species of animals indulge in loving under all circumstances. Actually, it is that simple.

Q: How can one see through a few undesirable things in a relationship?

A: Seeing through is a conscious task which is done in the situation, where your partner is behaving, speaking, or acting in a manner, that you do not expect. In that situation, it is normal if your mind becomes judgemental and reactive. But here is the catch. When you get into a normal pattern of judging and reacting, you are unable to see what your partner wanted from you. Your partner expects a particular thing, and when it doesn't happen, it makes him or her speak unfavourably.

At that point, your partner finds it difficult to convey his or her need in a nice manner. But it is your responsibility towards your own self to see through those words and reactions of your partner, so as to understand his or her actual need. If you do so, you will become aware of that need, and thereafter, when you do the needful, everything will turn in your favour.

At times, your mind may think that your partner does not value all that you have done for him or her, but it is not true. Your partner notes everything. Maybe your partner does not know how to acknowledge your efforts, but that does not mean he or she does not know those things about you. You need to have faith in your own self and your partner. It will help you to see through and act in the right direction, instead of getting stuck with the words.

Q: What is the proper way to ask for something?

A: Most people are apprehensive to ask for what they want. They expect their partners to be aware of how they want to be loved. As if their partner has some sort of mystical power 'to know the unsaid.' This is a common problem in all relationships. Nobody can read your mind. Others can only guess. And guesswork has a very low probability of 'being correct.'

You may wonder, "How do my parents and my friends do so many things without my asking them?" The answer is that it took them many years to get to know you. And it is only now that they know so much about you. But there were probably many discussions that happened through the years to get to this stage.

You may find certain people who coincidently do a lot of things that you do. Still, this is just a coincidence. The funny part is that even if you had married any of them, you would have still needed to ask them for help for a lot of things. Loving truly also includes asking for what you need. Some people think that there is no fun if one gets something by asking for it. This is a very wrong notion.

Asking for something on time means that you are loyal to your partner. Of course, you need to ask in a loving manner. Later in this book, you will learn a step-by-step way that you can use to ask for help. So make a commitment that you will ask for what you need, instead of waiting for a lifetime thinking that your partner will know your needs without you talking about them.

Q: How should one be grateful in a relationship?

A: It is very important that you regard the presence of your partner. You need to consciously receive the act of love that your partner extends to you. Taking love for granted is a very common mistake. It is important to observe everything that your partner does for you, instead of focussing on all the things that your partner is not able to do.

When you value your partner's act of love, you will feel thankful, and you will acknowledge it verbally. This gesture will make all the difference to your partner. Lack of positive acknowledgement is the biggest cause of problems between couples.

When the individuals in a couple do not acknowledge each other's positive gestures, each starts feeling that all their effort is useless. This leads to frustration and thereafter, fights. Therefore, make a commitment to yourself that you will receive the good that your partner does unto you. Reward him or her verbally and also in acts of love that are expected from your end.

Only good practice of all that you have learnt till now will ensure your readiness for the steps that follow.

CHAPTER
Twenty Two

Loving Truly – Seeing the Self in the Other

Till now, hundreds of instances must have occurred in your relationship. Some appeared pleasant to your mind, some unpleasant, some created confusion and ambiguity, some created anger, some created sadness and despair, some surprise, and so on. Whenever you experienced difficult times, you felt a lack of love. Didn't you? Do you not think that your partner must have also experienced a lack of love, in the same way?

Now that you have learnt that you need to take ownership of your relationship, is it not your responsibility to proactively create love in the relationship? Yes! It is. It is not about your romantic efforts, more about the true sense of love that you need to create in the relationship. The fact that difficult situations occur in relationships is normal, but if there is love, both of you can deal with any challenging situation very easily. The relationship that has love as a central pillar is called a 'love-strong relationship.'

Later, you will learn how to resolve issues and solve problems. But if your relationship is not a 'love-strong relationship', no amount of problem- solving can help. Love must not be dependent on any circumstance around both of you. If you start establishing the culture of creating love proactively, your partner will also start loving you in the same manner. Hence, make a commitment to your own self that you will learn these aspects well.

Q: How does one value a relationship?

A: It is very important to acknowledge the positive aspects of your partner's personality. The times you are upset with your partner, you lose sight of the positive aspects of your partner and of the relationship. It becomes important to take a few moments to think about selected positive aspects of your partner's personality. To start with, you can begin identifying between three and five distinguishing things about your partner that you find really pleasing.

Even if these qualities are only slightly evident at times, it is very important to note them. You may write those things on a piece of paper. Think about the respective incidents when you witnessed those qualities. When you describe those qualities to your partner, with reference to specific situations, he or she will admire you for saying them. It may appear very new to you, but deep down your partner needs to be valued. Everyone needs to be valued. Also, if you are comfortable, you can also ask your partner to describe the qualities in you as well.

Q: Why Do We Need Acknowledgement?

A: On a daily basis, if the individuals in a couple acknowledge each other's gestures, they will acquire a positive regard for each other. **Positive**

regard is a big determinant of love. To acquire it, you need to mention every big or small thing that your partner does for you.

Acknowledgement is not new to you. You definitely acknowledge the attendant in a restaurant, when he serves you your dish the way you expect. So why not acknowledge your own partner, who loves you day in and day out? Maybe you do not have the habit of acknowledging your own people. But there are many things that your partner does, that must be acknowledged.

You can do this is **four simple steps**.

1. The first step is to **tell your partner what he or she did for you**. It may be small or big, but you need to specify it.

2. The second step is to **share how you felt because that thing that was done for you**. When you describe 'how you felt', the other realises how important it is to you. You need to mention the feeling in words and not just use clichéd words like *happy* or *nice* or *good*. A few examples of words that describe feelings are – "I felt important, special, needed, wanted, loved, acknowledged, understood."

3. The third step is to **mention the impact that gesture had on you.** You can speak about the new belief that was formed in your mind

because of that gesture. These statements can start with the words "*It makes me believe that...*" or "Now I believe that..." It has to be explained in an affirmative manner in terms of the good that is happening now. Please don't explain in terms of what is not happening now. For example, say *"Now I can trust you more."* Do not say *"Now the mistrust has gone."* The two statements have a different impact.

4. The last step is to **tell the other what you can do for the other because of that gesture**. This is the reward for the other that he or she must know. Acknowledging acts of love this way creates a sense of love between partners. When you share in this fashion, the other will also start acknowledging your efforts.

Q: What should we do to fulfil our wish?

A: Ideally, the first task that a couple must do is to establish a sound knowledge of each other's likes, dislikes, aspirations, dreams, pain areas, and feel good factors. Only when you know them, you can begin to do those things for the other. It is obvious that energy doesn't get destroyed or wasted, it just changes form. So will your efforts for your partner. You need to be proactive in doing things that your partner needs or expects from you.

This proactiveness is a very powerful predictor of relationship stability. To do this, take the opportunity to build a detailed map of your partner's mind. You need to know about your partner's history, concerns, preferences, and his or her current world. You can casually ask open-ended questions. Your partner may give elaborate answers on few questions. He or she may give subtle hints about the answer to the other questions. Some answers may be restricted to a simple "Yes" or "No." It is very important to believe those answers and act accordingly.

When your partner is sharing his or her views, you may not think the same way as your partner. For example, if your partner mentions that politics is full of hypocrisy, remember it is about your partner's world. You may have your own understanding and preferences but loving is about loving the way the other wants to be loved. You do not need to have the same beliefs as they do. But surely, you can ensure that your partner is not forced to watch a political debate on television. If politics interests you, you are not expected to refrain yourself. You need to create a central route that ensures the comfort of your partner.

You need to love your partner the best you can. If there are things that you are not capable of doing but you are willing to, your partner will value you for them because he or she will sense your intent. Never reject or disapprove your partner. Nobody can take rejection or criticism, however incorrect he or she may be. You need approval and so does your partner. Giving your partner approval is about respecting his or her thoughts, feelings, and aspirations. This is loving your partner.

Q: How Do You Prove to Someone that You Care?

A: No matter how important other relationships may be, all of them exist in your life for a limited time, and they have a limited scope. Only your partner will be there for you forever. Your parents, children, siblings are all very important, but they have a limited role.

Primacy is about making the other feel that the relationship with him or her is PRIME. Giving **primacy** to your relationship with your partner is like an investment plan that definitely pays. It means placing the relationship in a slightly higher place of importance compared to other relationships. This does not mean that other relationships are not important.

When you were a student, you had to give primacy to your education. However, you did not have to have to abandon your parents, friends, or your hobbies to do that. Similarly, when you started your career, you gave your career primacy. Now as you begin the journey of your marriage, you have to give it primacy as well.

It is about knowing, feeling, and showing that your partner is most important.

At the same time, it is important that you give due attention to your family, friends, and other office colleagues. Establishing primacy is making a circle that has a permissible boundary. The couple stays inside this circle of primacy. And other people who are important are allowed to come in at all times. But you need to remember that they come and go.

The boundary explains primacy for the partner. You don't need to be blunt in establishing this boundary. Be careful not to make any gestures that make others feel discriminated against. Do it gracefully or in a jestful or jovial manner such that other people find it comfortable in accepting the primacy. If your folks are wise, they will understand the boundary. If someone is not wise enough, then you have to be a little assertive in establishing the primacy.

Let us understand a few gestures and examples that are helpful in establishing the primacy—

- Whenever other people ask you to make a decision, **look at your spouse and make eye contact with the aim of seeking your partner's input**. This way, your partner will feel his or her primacy and so will others. Whether the decision is small or big, maintaining primacy is a must.

- **Whenever you accomplish something**, regardless of its significance, whether less or more, **acknowledge your partner's role in attributing to that success.** This will make your partner feel prime.
- **Be with your spouse in public gatherings**. Ensure that your partner is never alone in any public gathering unless he or she wants to attend some function alone.
- **Giving and getting your spouse due importance in a group or in private** is very important.
- Whenever your partner needs your help, **listening** to him or her establishes the primacy.

These are a few ways to establish primacy, but there can be many other ways that you can use to express primacy. Although doing these things does not require much effort, if not done, they make your partner feel unwanted.

Generally, when you are amongst others, it is very likely that you will forget to give your partner primacy, but you need to keep it in mind. If you establish primacy for your partner in the eyes of your family members, they will also start respecting and acknowledging your partner in the same way that you do.

Q: How does one take a stand in a relationship?

A: A friend in need is a friend indeed.

This statement holds true even in your relationship with your partner. Love is created the most in times of need. Fair weather friends are many but the one who stands beside you in a time of need is most remembered. So if you support your partner, if someone is criticising him or her, in your presence or even behind your back, it is a test of your love. Your parents or siblings or friends may end up criticising your partner intentionally or unintentionally.

Obviously, if it some outsider, you will stand up for your partner, without wasting a second. But the challenge is when it is your close one doing wrong to your partner. You have to stand up for your partner while recognising that close one's concern. When you are there for your partner, the respect your partner has for you will increase multifold. This too contributes to 'creating love.' The disconnect between your partner and others is because of a difference in thinking. It is normal.

However, even if your partner has done something undesirable, you have to take your partner's side at that moment. It is tricky because it is your family member on the other side, who is also important to you. So you need to acknowledge his or her point of view as well while acknowledging the possibility of a mistake from your partner's end. Still, it should convey to everyone that you are on your partner's side. This way, you create love. You should refrain from correcting your partner in front of others, under any circumstance. However, a later time, you can discuss the situation with your partner. You need to do it in privacy, in a closed room.

The subsequent parts of the book will help you learn the way to resolve problems – it is called *The Connection Talk.*

If you practice all that you have learnt till now, you will become capable of creating a happy and love-filled relationship.

CHAPTER
Twenty Three
Learning to Communicate

Despite having the right concept of love and the commitment to love, there can be issues between the two of you. This is normal. It happens because there are two people who are involved. Two people have two different worlds that they live in.

Two different worlds mean that they have different values, expectations, likes, and dislikes. Values are ideals that guide or qualify your personal conductand interaction with the world. They help you decide what is right and wrong. They inform you about 'your conduct in life.' It is rare that all the values between two people match completely.

It is also normal for both of you to carry different sets of expectations from your relationship. These expectations may centre on how your marriage should be, what your partner should do for you, how your partner should behave with you, etc. These expectations begin forming right from your teenage days. Most people either do not express their emotions, assuming that their partner already knows them on their own or they explode and express themselves in irrational ways. Both these ways lead to fights and arguments.

In the following part of the book, you will learn the right way to express your expectations. Additionally, it is important to have realistic expectations from the other. Your mind may reject and rebel at this statement. Maybe you think that your partner must do those things, but just think for a while, can he or she really do them? If you put yourself in his or her shoes, do you think it is really that easy and comfortable to do those things from that position?

Put yourself in his or her position yourself and then decide. It is wiser to first empathise with the other, and then on that basis, create a new set of expectations that are more realistic. Your mind may oppose this and think that your partner should also empathise with you. When you are not able to become one team with your partner, any issue can trigger a fight. Only when the both of you act as a team, you can resolve issues together.

You must have heard people saying *"Marriage is an Institution."* Have you ever thought why the word *institution* is used?" An institution is a place where two or more people cohabit to learn something. Marriage is an institution, where a couple lives together to learn to love and form a united team.

Both of you need to help each other fulfil your respective needs. There are no wrong and right needs. Only when you know each other's worlds, you become capable of creating central solutions. In reality, all problems are a manifestation of some unmet need.

So let us first understand the **Ground Rules to Problem-Solving.**

These rules facilitate trouble-free problem-solving. They need to be observed with discipline. Problems become complex when these rules are not observed.

Whenever there is an issue, you have to refrain from **three ineffective ways of handling a problem**. You do not have to withdraw. You do not have to get in the attack-and-defend mode. You do not have to come into a state of confluence.

Let us understand these **Wrong Ways To Handle A Problem—**

1. **First Wrong Way - Withdrawal**

   When a couple does not talk about a problem at hand and bury their heads in the sand like ostriches, it is called *withdrawal.* They pretend to others and themselves that the problem does not exist. It leads to a dysfunctional relationship. At the face of it, everyone thinks that there is no problem with the couple. But in reality, they start living separate lives.

   As they want to avoid confrontations, they end up avoiding any interaction around the topic of disconnect. But a great deal of discontent and resentment starts building up, which explodes one day like a time bomb. This wrong approach does not solve the problem but adds fuel to the fire. Both of them feel rejected and start growing apart.

2. **Second Wrong Way – Attack-and-Defend Game**

   In this pattern, the couple does not talk about the problem all the time. But whenever they encounter a difficulty, one of them points out the mistake of the other and the other defends himself or herself. They exchange turns into attacking and defending, eventually creating an environment of fights, arguments, and tension in the house all the time. Other members also suffer because of this pattern.

Some couples go into the mode of isolation. They create inflexible boundaries and the minute either of them tries to discuss or force his or her input around the problem, they start arguing using sarcastic words and a high pitch. With this wrong pattern, couples get accustomed to the mechanism of answering back. This pattern leads to a lot of frustration, angry outbursts, and disgust.

3. **Third Wrong Way - Confluence**

   In this pattern, the couple does not talk about the problem—one of them just gives in and comes into compliance at the surface level. In this method, one of the partners lets his or her personality get shadowed by the other. This is done to temporarily avoid conflicts. So he or she starts doing exactly what the other wants. The other doesn't get to know that there is suppressed anguish in the relationship.

   The other never gets to know that it was just false acceptance to avoid fights, until the day there is a blast, because this wrong pattern also does not work for too long. For a long time, the dominating partner continues to think that he or she has successfully established the "my way or highway."

They live in an illusion that everything is going perfectly. It's like being unaware of a punctured tyre while driving at top speed. The car goes great for some time. But the inevitable happens one day. The car either topples or catches fire.

It is important to put an end to all these three dysfunctional ways of dealing with the problem.

Q: How do I understand my partner better?

A: Knowing each other's world means knowing everything about the problem. You need to do it step-by-step. One of you can begin by sharing your worlds. It is called *The Connection Talk*. In *The Connection Talk*, both of you share your situation completely.

It involves knowing—

- The presenting problem as seen by you,
- The deeper reasons behind a problem,
- The impact of the problem on you,
- The possible solutions according to you,
- Your offering if those solutions are accepted.

When you both share your worlds this way, arriving at solutions becomes very easy.

Q: How to solve problems in a relationship?

A: Your mind may think that your problem is too complicated and that finding a solution is very tough. It also thinks that it will take a lot of energy and time to explain to your partner because you have tried it so many times. But there is a catch. Only because your mind is already preoccupied with all these thoughts, you experience difficulty in your relationship.

As a result, you could never relate to your partner and vice versa. Both of you sense each other's mental image. You need to refrain from these negative images about your partner and your relationship. Having faith in yourself, in your love, and in your partner will surely turn everything in your favour.

Q: How does one go about solving problems in a relationship?

A: Finding and applying solutions is the easiest task but finding the right solutions call for an understanding of the actual problem. If you are committed to unite with your partner and to discover a mutually acceptable solution, solutions will definitely surface. Do you know that every problem has a solution? Problems arise every day. Even when you were single, you had problems every day, but you knew you had to resolve them.

Similarly, you need to resolve the problems in your relationship as well. In fact, you need to discover solutions every day. To this end, you need to be committed and proactive to unite with your partner, to discover a solution. The minute you keep this in your mind, you will see that your partner also begins responding in the same way. You need to know that it was your intent to unite with your partner that was missing—and the presence of that is what your partner is now sensing.

Q: How important is the place and time while discussing relationship issues?

A: Not doing anything about problems has never benefitted anyone. You need to sit together in private, comfortable space, where there is no disturbance. Sitting down specifically to discuss the issues in the right way always helps. This makes the other believe that you value him or her, and you have the right intent. For this, you need to be open to the other's world, both from your mind and your heart. Only when you are open from within, your partner will be able to feel the same towards you.

Your tone of voice must be comforting and collaborative. It should not be formal or under any pressure. You both need to share your worlds, one by one, starting with one particular issue. It is irrelevant who starts first because the problem is common to both of you. The source of the problem is the differentness in each of your views on that particular issue. When your partner starts sharing, you need to zip your mouth until he or she has completed.

You will feel the urge to correct the other. Almost everyone commits this mistake, it is normal. You need to bring the focus back to what the other is saying. Because if you chip in, the other may start to defend himself or herself or go silent. Also, he or she will get to know that you do not value what is being shared. Please hold yourself back. Keep your points in mind and discuss them later. Your job is to first understand the other completely. If you refrain from chipping in, there is a great probability that your questions will get answered on their own, while the other is sharing. Once the other has completed sharing, you need to acknowledge all that other has said exactly the way they said it.

'Acknowledgement' means that you tell the other that you understand what the other has said. This is done so as to give the other an opportunity to know that you have understood it correctly. Ask the other if you have understood everything correctly or not. Maybe the other wants to add or correct something. And then you have to share your views about the same problem using the same steps. You will both be able to find out the solutions very easily if you connect in that particular manner.

Q: How should our tone and words be while discussing relationship issues?

A: The conversation must be held with an aim at making you both good friends who help each other resolve issues and create central routes. As a friend, you need to be very careful that you do not directly or indirectly blame your partner, his or her thoughts, or his or her people.

You need to speak without referring to the other. Whenever you have to mention something that other has done, instead of directly saying that you did this, refer to the action instead of directly putting the onus on the person. Your words and tone should reflect that you are a friend.

Q: How does one propose possible solutions to difficulties in a relationship?

A: After you have shared your worlds, propose solutions. Remember that when you propose solutions, the other should not feel compelled; you need to accept your solutions in the exact way that you have thought about it. Maybe the solution that you propose is not applicable in the eyes of the other. You have to be your partner's friend, and friends do not push. Friends do not dominate.

At the same time, if your partner proposes a solution, you need to respect and thank him or her for the idea. What is more important is the intention to make the other feel comfortable and supported. Some problems take time to get solved. Some solutions are not immediately applicable. Some proposed solutions trigger other ideas that may be even more beneficial. So be open, supportive, and accommodative while creating central routes.

Connecting Talk

Communication is all about **asking for all that you need** and **knowing what the other needs**.

"*You are*" and the "World also *is*." This means you exist in this world. The world and you are interconnected and thereby, interdependent. You cannot exist in isolation from the world. So it is very important to acknowledge and respect this interconnectedness. You are connected to all the people who are related to you, and even to people who are not related to you. All people matter, and they have an impact on your being, that is, you.

When you are connected to all the people, there will be transactions with these people. Transactions mean that you have some work or dependency on these people and vice versa. Similarly, you are dependent on your partner as well. Your partner's support is critical in all the phases of your life. So you need to ask your partner for help. At the second level, you need to know what your partner wants from you.

Q: Is it important to ask for help?

A: Your mind may rebel and ask, "*Why should I ask for help?*"

Here is the answer.

The human mind, by default, feels the need to help. But only those who get an opportunity to help become ready to help. Maybe you have never asked for help in the way the other expects.

In your present situation, if you need support from your partner, you need to use a step-by-step method, as follows:

1. You have to invite your partner, for a discussion. To this effect, you can say to him or her, "I have something to share with you. When can we talk?"

2. As a response, your partner may ask you to talk it out then and there. As this discussion is a power talk, it must be done at a specific time when the other can comfortably listen to you without any distraction.

   The discussion must happen at some place where there is no distraction. If the place you are both at is convenient enough, you can have the discussion in the same place. Otherwise, decide on a comfortable time and place, considering your partner's convenience. This power talk will have its impact only when the place is convenient to both of you.

   Even making a cup of tea has to be done in a particular way, which when deviated from, results in a poor taste. Isn't it? If you follow these steps in the right order, you will get magical results. Getting anything from anyone will become very easy for you. Of course, the other person must have the ability to do that thing. Even if the other does not have the ability to, at least he or she will be able to relate to you in terms of that situation.

3. Now when you have expressed your need, your partner will share his or her response with you. You need to be flexible and open to receiving whatever your partner has to say. It is possible that your partner may agree fully, partially, or in some other way. So be ready to negotiate and arrive at a solution that is agreeable to the two of you, instead of expecting the solution to be exactly as you wish.

4. Also, if your partner needs some time to respond, give your partner an opportunity to respond, as per his or her comfort. He or she may need some time to respond in your favour. Trust that there will be a gradual change. Be empathetic towards with your partner because all this is new for him or her as well.

It is possible that your partner may not react with a lot of warmth or speak in exactly the same tone as you were speaking. But be happy about the fact that for the first time, you have planted a new seed of thought in your partner's mind. Have faith in yourself and in your partner. And you will surely witness the result in your favour. The result may not be the way you expect, but you will be in a better position because of this power talk.

CHAPTER
Twenty Four
Connecting Spiritually with Your People

Marriage is not only about your relationship with your partner. It is also abouyour relationship with your partner's family of origin – the extended family or in-laws. To some extent, it is also about the relationship between your family and your partner's family. Therefore, it is very important that you and your partner ensure that all these other relationships also get ample importance. Both of you need to play your respective roles in your families. To do this, you need help from your partner, in order to create the right image of yourself in the eyes of your in-laws.

When your spouse and you fail to provide this help, it impacts the marriage. Also, as a couple, both of you need to establish the identity of a new sub-family, in your larger family. This needs to be done to build a sense of autonomy for your sub-family. When your new family does not get the autonomy it needs, the marriage starts getting choked by the larger family. So when it comes to your family as well, if your partner complains about issues regarding your parents, you need to play your role well. You need to learn the deeper realities and ways to create the right environment at your home.

The disconnect between you and your in-laws can become a very natural source of conflict in your relationship. The situation is likewise for your partner. Greater than the trouble that you face with your in-laws, is your inability to create a connection with them. A thought may surface, "*I have tried my best, but I still am not able to remove the disconnect. This is impacting my relationship with my partner.*" However, there is a solution.

Q: How does one have a positive image of in-laws?

A: However positively you think, your friends, relatives, and society, jokingly paint a negative image of the IN-LAWS in your mind, from a very early age. This negative image is registered at the subconscious level. It is not only about your in-laws, you carry this over-generalised image about all authority figures, like police officers, school principals, and others who have some authority. It is untrue that all police officers or school principals are strict, and the logic applies when it comes to your in-laws as well.

This preconceived image of the in-laws is so strong that the person starts judging, perceiving, and behaving so negatively that it turns into reality. The person is not able to see the other good things about the in-laws. All of this happens subconsciously. So most wives end up saying, "I didn't want dominating in-laws, but God didn't spare me," and most husbands say, "I never wanted interfering in-laws, and but my in-laws interfere a lot, and they take care of my wife so much that it disturbs my marriage." Now this question may arise, "*When I am doing nothing, why do my in-laws give me so much trouble?*"

True, you may not be doing anything, but your thoughts can be read through your facial expressions, and the other person reacts accordingly. Others' reactions may be minute but when your mind connects those reactions to the preconceived image, it gets that evidence. And then, the snowball effect comes into action. This can be explained with this example—the way a small snowflake begins rolling from the mountain top and finally turns into a giant snowball, your thoughts too turn into reality. This does not mean that it is only your fault; surely there are other causes as well. You will learn about them in the latter part of the book.

It is very important to know that your in-laws are a core part of your partner's family, who have been there for your partner for decades, just like your parents, who have been there for you all these years. You cannot see your partner in isolation from his or her family. If you accepted your partner, you need to accept their partner as well. If your partner belongs to you, his or her family also belongs to you. Instead of letting your mind exaggerate other things, start telling yourself "*They are important and they belong to me.*" Saying this to yourself will help.

Q: What is the way to establish trust in the eyes of one's in-laws?

A: It is important to remember that you are a new member in your partner's family. Keeping that in mind, you need to acknowledge this family as your family. To do this, you need to have a sense of ownership towards this new family of yours. But when this does not happen, things start becoming difficult for them and for you as well. You need to help them by doing certain things so that they can trust you. You should help them because they belong to you.

Do you sometimes think that your in-laws are overly critical of you? If so, think about it for a while. Why do they carry this image of you? Maybe you did certain things against their wishes and you didn't do something that they wanted? It all depends on what image you create in their heart. The first step for you is to create the right image of your in-laws in your mind. Only when you do this, you will able to do those things that make them like you. The only way out is to have a positive approach.

To accomplish this, you need to do your homework well. You need to understand their culture, rituals, and beliefs as much as you can. You cannot afford to be the odd person out. If you reject, criticise, or argue about their thoughts and beliefs, then they can never like you. Think of your best friends. You like them because they understand you and support you. There may be certain things that they think differently about. Yet, you like your best friends because they always support you, even if they do not do the same things as you do. Likewise, you need to be that best friend to your in-laws.

You need to support them and only then, they will begin to take a liking to you. Soon a day will come when they begin supporting you as well. For this, you need to first know the objective of doing all this. All this is very significant to your life, your relationship, and your future. Start telling your mind your in-laws are yours, and that you have to make good friends out of them. Find out a few common areas of interests, likes, and dislikes. You can try to spend as much time as you can, together with them, doing those common activities.

You need to remember that you cannot fake it. The idea is to mingle with them. If you find it difficult to do all this, ask your partner to help you. To begin with, you can spend time with your in-laws along with your partner and slowly start doing it on your own. If you live away from your in-laws, at least try to connect with them over the phone. And whenever you get to meet them, spend time with them and compensate.

Q: How can one establish a sub-family within a larger family?

A: Almost all couples remain unaware of the concept of the sub-family within the larger family. This leads to disgust between them. A unique sub-family of the boy and the girl needs to exist within the larger family. It is like a smaller circle that exists in the larger circle. The problem arises when the existence of this sub-family is not acknowledged by the larger family. This happens either because the boy or girl lacks awareness about this.

Sometimes, it also happens because of the parents. Some parents who are authoritarians do not believe in giving their children autonomy. At the outset, they look very nice and they are good indeed. They have good intentions but they interfere with big and small things alike. Children in some families lack assertiveness. When a boy or a girl in such a family grows up and gets married, it is impossible for the new, unique family to get the much needed unique identity. As a result, the new member who joins does not get the respect they deserve.

Also such parents, at an unconscious level, fear losing control over their child. And in this pursuit, they try to dominate their child's spouse as well. All of this happens subconsciously. They do not want to do it consciously. At the same time, their child is no more a child. He or she has grown up and has his or her personal identity. In this case, he or she needs to respectfully assert the uniqueness of his or her sub-family.

Similarly, you too need to establish the fact that your sub-family is unique and the respect it gets important to you. This way, when you respect your unique family, i.e., your partner and yourself, things will start to get better. In the beginning, you have a very important role to play in terms of orienting your partner to your larger family and vice versa. This is similar to the orientation of new employees in a company or a new student in a college. Facilitate healthy acceptance of your partner within your larger family. You also have to play the role of a guardian.

You have to treat your partner with grace in front of your parents and vice versa. Praise them in front of each other. If you need to correct your partner or the family members that are part of your larger family, do it in private. All this is similar to the concept of primacy that you have learnt in the previous part in the book.

In this case, it is a little different because this concept of a sub-family needs to be facilitated for a healthy relationship. There will be transactions between your partner and your family members. If you have done the best that you can, you need to ask your parents and your partner help to establish this sub-family within the larger family. You have learnt how to ask for help in the previous part – *Connection Talk.*

Q: How do I take a stand for my partner?

A: Whenever your family of origin is criticising your partner, subtly stop them and protect your partner, even if your partner is doing wrong. You can definitely convey the things that your partner needs to work on, but do it later and in private. If you stand in support of your partner, you will be in a position to explain the views of your people to your partner as well.

You also need to go back and talk to your family members and let them know the real situation. Use The Connection Talk to ask for their help, which will help maintain their respectful positions and yours. This also needs to be done in private and not in the presence of your partner.

When you support your partner during the tough times, you create an opportunity for yourself, to recommend the right strategy to resolve the issue. If you do not feel you are powerful enough to get your partner the respect he or she deserves, you are creating a big problem for your relationship. This is because if you continue this way, you will lose respect in the eyes of your partner. You can use The Connection Talk and solve this problem by talking to your parents.

Q: How Do You Get Respect from Your Family?

A: If your family members always criticise you in front of your partner, it is very important to stop this. You need to be assertive. You need to let your parents know that you are an adult who is capable of handling things.

Q: How does one become less dependent on parents?

A: When you are in a marriage, your partner is your prime family. You are not supposed to share everything with your parents. You need to become completely self-dependent. The more you share with your parents, the more opportunities they get to give you their opinion. Even though they do it out of concern, it is detrimental to your relationship.

Your partner and you should have the autonomy to make life decisions. But when you are dependent on your parents, it will appear as interference to your partner. This does not mean that you should be secretive. However, you can avoid giving complete details to your parents.

Sometimes, some family members like elder siblings, elder sibling's spouses, uncles, and aunts become quite close. Being close and sharing deep relationships is alright. But some people become completely dependent and share even the smallest detail about their personal life with those family members. It is alright until one gets married. But you need to realise that after marriage, your partner needs to be given this primacy. Not because you are answerable to your partner, but because you have to create this special bond. It does not mean that you are selfish and cutting off ties with your people who have been there for so many years.

All relationships are unique and everyone needs all of those relationships always. It is just that you have to grow to next stage of life and build this new family with your spouse. All animals observe this natural principle of life. If your family members are not mature enough, they may feel that you have changed and have become selfish. In such a case, you need to use The Connection Talk to make them aware of your position.

Q: How can you help build a positive relationship between your partner and your parents?

A: It is obvious that your partner needs time to establish a bond with your folks. Empathise with your partner, and let him or her take the time to establish the needed connection. To achieve this, you need to appreciate your partner for all the efforts that he or she puts in to build that connection. The same is applicable to your partner's family as well. Your partner also needs to help you connect to his or her family.

Both of you have a joint responsibility as well. You need to form a team with each other to ensure that your respective families also respect each other. Neither family is superior in any form after the wedding. Both need to treat each other with equal respect. Both of you have to facilitate the necessary orientation between the respective families. Do the best you can to foster a sense of acceptance between the two families. Problems are sure to arise when both of you do not play your roles well.

Q: How does one solve problems between mothers-in-law and daughters-in-law?

A: The 'mother-in-law and daughter-in-law conflict' has been prevalent in marriages since the beginning of time. It is a reality in most marriages, to this day. It happens in marriages when basic awareness about role conflicts is not established. Neither woman is bad. Neither wants to see fights and problems in their home. It is the conflict of the roles that creates the tussle between them. Let us understand what role-conflict is and why it happens. It all stems from **Role Confusion.**

The problem between the mother-in-law and daughter-in-law is born out of this Role Confusion. The mother was the caretaker of the boy and the whole family for more than two-and-a-half decades. Suddenly, a new girl comes in. In all marriages, both women begin with a positive mindset. At the same time, they have zero clarity on *who will do what*. This ambiguity starts from small issues like managing the kitchen to the laundry, to big issues like buying a house. This ambiguity in the change of roles may even happen when it comes to small things like whether the living room needs a new curtain. It is like having two managers in one office.

It is the boy's job (i.e., the husband) to respectfully negotiate the roles for both women. When he fails to negotiate the roles, both resort to their own irrational ways of gaining control. This confusion manifests in fights, even if the new couple lives separate from the family.

The sad part is that neither woman wins this game of gaining control. In this situation, all the parties lose. It is because the boy does not know that he needs to establish clarity in the roles. As a result, the mother ends up being uncomfortable in giving away the control. The daughter-in-law also becomes a bit inflexible in terms of assuming a different role, she wants full control instead. The boy has to assertively mediate and put an end to this confusion. To effectively do this, he needs to be mature enough not to take sides.

The boy needs to assure his mother and his wife that he intends to spend time with both of them. He needs to define that time very subtly and righteously. It is obvious that he needs to spend much more time with his wife. At the same time, he can allocate time for his parents as well.

Even if the couple lives away from the family and meets them every now and then, the boy still needs to balance his time in the same way. The wife has her role as well. She also needs to accept that her mother-in-law has raised her husband for a long time, so it is difficult for her to suddenly accept the change. It is uncomfortable for her as well. Yet, she needs to seek help from her husband in a very accommodating manner to establish the autonomous functioning of the new sub-family in this larger family.

When both the husband and wife play their roles well, it becomes easy for everybody to accept the change. You need to accept the fact this may take some time. You can use The Connection Talk with your family members and your partner to ensure that they understand. You also need to be prepared to co-create central routes. There are no fixed rules in relationships. Relationships are about relating to the other. Only when you consciously take the first step in relating to the other, you will receive love from the other in return.

CHAPTER *Twenty Five*

Experiencing Spiritual Union and Attaining Fulfilment in Relationships

By now, you have learnt almost everything that is needed to create a happy relationship. In this part, you will learn about intimacy at two levels - emotional and physical.

First of all, you need to know the answer to this — **What is Intimacy?**

Intimacy is closeness. This closeness is essential to the growth of a relationship. If a couple is not emotionally close, they end up living passively, like two strangers in a train journey.

You also need to know **What Makes Intimacy Fade**.

Most relationships that fail have very little or no intimacy at all. Most relationships have **'Pseudo-Intimacy.' 'Pseudo'** means **pretentious**. Couples who have pseudo-intimacy please each other superficially. If given a chance, they will not do anything for each other. They portray a fake niceness towards each other, which does not work for too long. And when they stop doing good things, they end up telling each other, "You have changed. You were not like this earlier. Had I known this, I would have never married you."

It creates chaos, which continues for long years. And finally, a stage comes when they realise their partner will not change. They remain completely clueless about the solution. They do not know what to do. Owing to social pressure, they either compromise throughout their lives or quit. If you do not want to get into this trap of pseudo-intimacy, you need to learn more about authentic intimacy.

There are **two levels of intimacy in a relationship – Emotional Intimacy** and **Physical Intimacy**

You need to establish the right concept of emotional intimacy. **Emotional intimacy is about being close to the other's emotions and true feelings**. In the previous parts of the book, you have learnt ways to know, accept, and support each other's worlds.

Only when you are emotionally close, you will discover the sameness and differentness among the two of you. And then, you will be able to connect and form one united team. This team can then be called a 'couple.' The term 'couple' is used a lot in physics. It may be defined as 'Two different parts fitting together to make something new.' This is a conscious task that needs to be done jointly by both of you. Of course, you cannot be emotionally intimate throughout the day because you have a relationship with your being, as well. It is equally important to have your own personal space.

Levels of intimacy tend to vary at different times in the day. The way you cannot expect yourself to be happy and excited the whole day, your partner will also have different levels of intimacy at different points in time.

The **second form** of intimacy is **physical intimacy**. The term **physical intimacy** signifies **tangible closeness** between a couple. This intimacy is generally understood as sexual intimacy. Even though sexual intimacy plays an integral part in a relationship, it is only a small part of physical intimacy.

Physical intimacy in a relationship is a direct reflection of the emotional intimacy between couples. This is like a cycle because physical intimacy nurtures the emotional bonding between the couple. Both partners need to understand each other's needs and see what best they can do to ensure mutual satisfaction. The key to this is communication. Most couples do not have a comfortable discussion on this topic. Talking about physical intimacy is always challenging for those who do not discuss other issues openly either.

You need to use The Connection Talk to communicate your needs to your partner, and also to know your partner's needs. Once you do this, both of you can jointly create a great intimate life. Most societies do not promote open discussions centering sexuality and sensuality. This leads to a lack of awareness and thereby, a lack of physical intimacy between a couple. However educated and modern you and your partner may be, there is a possibility that both of you are unaware of this very important aspect of a relationship.

Furthermore, when couples do not connect on the aspect of physical intimacy, they start losing attraction. Lack of attraction makes people doubt whether their partner loves them or not. Sometimes, when people have reached the last thread, they find a lot of difficulty in acknowledging their emotions and things turn bad.

Q: Why is knowledge of physical intimacy so important?

A: This problem exists in almost all societies. The education at the school level imparts biological knowledge about sex. However, concepts such as sensuality and love are not part of any course. It is because of this that people remain unaware throughout their lives. Physical intimacy, at a deeper level, is the need to explore the other gender. In the beginning of any relationship, both partners are willing to support each other to create pleasure and satisfaction.

But due to a lack of awareness, they use hit-and-trial methods, which in most cases, kills the objective. Only the right orientation leads to a positive outcome, which is—to create love. That is why the word sex was replaced 'lovemaking.' If you consider lovemaking the main goal and acquire the right awareness about your partner's concept of lovemaking, you make it easy for the both of you.

Q: How does one have realistic expectations around physical intimacy in a relationship?

A: In many cases, at least one of the partners have unrealistic expectations about physical intimacy within their marriage. These unrealistic expectations are built during teenage days, due to a variety of reasons. When these fantasies are not practical for the other, they remain unfulfilled, and the dissatisfaction that emanates creates a gap between the couple. It is important to have the right concept of physical intimacy.

Apart from the biological aspect of physical intimacy, love and a sense of togetherness are also very important. Judging the partner's expectations as unrealistic is not right. However, one must share his or her inability to fulfill that expectation. Firstly, both partners should have plenty of love between them, so they can create mutually acceptable solutions. The key is to create love and not to consider the expectation as right or wrong. You should definitely refrain from anything that leads to physical pain or emotional discomfort.

Q: Do different things trigger intimacy in men and women?

A: A man feels like he belongs and is accepted when he receives physical love from his woman. A woman gets turned on when she receives emotional love from her man. This works like a cycle, where both have to play their respective roles. It is important that both the partners are aware of this cycle. But here is the catch. Men think that the woman should play her role first, and the woman expects her man to play his role first. This irony exists in most relationships that lack physical intimacy.

Emotional love leads to physical love, which in turn leads to emotional love, and so the cycle continues. Those who are unable to keep this cycle running explore extramarital relationships. It is funny that those who go outside the marriage have to abide by the same principles of emotional and physical love as well, which if they had played righteously in their own relationship could have turned everything positive. So if you have played your role in your relationship well, you can definitely create great physical intimacy. It is a very simple logic that when applied well, works well and creates magic in the relationships.

Q: Is It Important to Be Attractive?

A: The word *attractiveness* originates from the concept of the magnet. A magnet has a latent capacity to attract. This means that the magnet has to be a magnet, if attraction is to occur. Similarly, one has to have a self that is attractive. This needs to be done at both the body level and the psychological level. Sexual attractiveness is a quality to be created both in the personality and the body.

Some men and women do not believe in THE enhancement of beauty in the body. They carry a strong opinion that they should be accepted the way they are. But this works completely against them. They argue that one need to be authentic. But at the same time, authenticity must be presented well. Even if you look at diamonds—a raw diamond is authentic, but only when it is given the perfect cut and shape, it is appreciated. It works similarly when it comes to food as well. A vegetable when cut and cooked well serves its purpose.

So is the case with physical intimacy. When you present your body well to your partner, it is also an act of love. Not working on sexual attractiveness sends repelling signals to your partner. Also, the same attractiveness needs to be worked on, in terms of the personality as well. All living species—be it insects, birds, or animals, or even flowers use this concept of attractiveness. More than being attractive, you need to feel attractive. Just the way you make an effort to dress up for a meeting, you can indulge in dressing up sensually and feeling sensual for your partner as well. Attractiveness triggers the need for intimacy in the other. The goal is to make the other want you, instead of you asking for him or her.

Q: How important is creativity in a relationship?

A: Intimacy is not just a task. Those who think it is a task end up repelling their partner. This leads to the death of physical intimacy in relationships. In a very short span of time, such thoughts lead to boredom in relationships. To avoid this, you have to create fun and excitement in your physical life. It is about triggering the need in each other to bring excitement. Creativity brings life. It shows that you are interested.

Do more of what works. Stop all that is not working. Keep trying new things. Do not think that physical intimacy is a daily chore. Making it a special experience is very important. The word *sensual* comes from the word senses. Physical intimacy needs to be a sensory experience instead of a five-minute task. You can work on the ambiance and make it a memorable occasion every day.

Q: Can Some Relationships Be Really Unique?

A: Do not aim at creating a super-unique experience. Mutual comfort and joy should be the aim. Do not wait for the perfectly comfortable situation to arrive. Stay calm, discuss, and just indulge in creating a good experience for each other. There is no ideal physical intimacy. If you experience some difficulty, seeking professional help is always a good idea. You should work as a team and refrain from any form of blame game.

Couples who are not emotionally bonded find difficulties in their sex lives as well. It is not a game that you have to win. It is about a partnership to create mutual satisfaction. The ultimate mantra is healthy discussions.

Q: How should one discuss intimacy issues?

A: As this is a sensitive topic, here are a few facts that you must keep in mind before you begin discussions on the subject of physical intimacy.

1. **First - Ensure Your Partner's Comfort with the Discussion**

   You need to be humble while you initiate a discussion on physical intimacy. Do not initiate a discussion just before or after being intimate. You can ask your partner for a specific time, considering his or her comfort. If your partner is not too comfortable discussing certain details about something, ensure that he or she does not feel pushed.

2. **Second – Do Not Joke or Pass Any Sarcastic Comments About Your Partner**

   Joking or being sarcastic while on the topic of physical intimacy is a blunder. Even indirect references to your partner can kill the objective of the discussion. You can use The Connection Talk to explain your requirement. It is not wise to mention any inability of your partner as it may prove to be a disaster. Every individual has a sexual self-esteem. Judging his or her sexual performance is a direct attack on the person's self-esteem.

3. **Third – Help Your Partner Build a Positive Sexual Self-Esteem**

   Appreciate your partner while discussing physical intimacy. There must be a lot of good things about your partner and your physical relationship that you can acknowledge. Physical intimacy is a sensitive topic. But if you mention the good aspects of your partner, of his or her body, the discussion can lead to fruitful results.

4. **Fourth – Avoid Arguments**

   You need to be extra cautious while discussing physical intimacy. Avoid arguments. If you get into heated arguments, it will have a negative impact on other aspects of your relationship as well. If you see that the discussion is not going in the right direction, be respectful and close the discussion with a lot of warmth.

5. **Fifth – Subtly Educate Your Partner If There Is Some Unawareness**

   If required, humbly share some information on sexuality or sensuality to your partner. You need to ensure that your partner does not feel too burdened or inferior. He or she should feel that you are accepting the lack of information as normal. You can also mention that you did not know anything earlier either.

The objective of discussion is to create a good relationship between the two of you. If your partner has a different view, be supportive and accommodative, instead of proving your point.

If you observe all these facts, you will easily create a great partnership in this aspect of your relationship as well.

PART *Six*

Tasting Success in Career

CHAPTER
Twenty Six

Witnessing the Gap

You need to first understand what's happening with you. Only when you know that, you can do something about it.

You may experience a low sense of self, but do you know that there is not a single person who has NOT experienced this situation at least once in their life. It is a different fact though, that your feelings may not be same as those experienced by others. Also, the impact of the situation appears big only to the person who experiences it. Nobody else can feel that impact exactly the way you are experiencing it.

For this let us understand this term *low self-esteem*.

Low means *less*.

Self means *yourself*,

And *esteem* comes from *estimation*, that is, the *qualitative evaluation*. Now a question arises.

Who is estimating your *Self* as low, and who is feeling low because of this estimation?

Your answer to this will be "My mind estimates my self-image as low, and I feel low." It is important to know that in between these two processes – the thinking and the evaluation, there is a subtle gap that you do not understand. This means that involuntary thoughts are going on in your mind that make you feel low about yourself. This happens because of a conditioning of your mind.

Have you noticed that some people are able to come out of this cycle of thinking and feeling very quickly? But you have been continually feeling less about your *self* for a long time. What goes differently for you? It is the conditioning of your mind that makes it more difficult for you.

Now another question arises—“But why to you and why this much?”

The answer is—it is the constant thinking that happens in the subconscious mind that makes it all different for you. Most of the time, people are not aware of these subconscious thoughts that finally turn into beliefs. Subsequently, these beliefs manifest in forming a sense of being less.

Q: Why do I have negative thoughts about myself ?

A: This is a critical factor that leads to feelings of low self and a lack of confidence. It is the mind that takes you into the cycle of self-blame and self-doubt, with regard to the life you have lived so far. Your mind has a habit of finding reasons to blame the self for every unfavourable thing that happens around you. This happens because you compare yourself with others, and this constant comparison creates an impact on you.

It is true that during a tough situation, people end up blaming themselves or others, even when they know that this blaming is illogical and damaging.

But constantly blaming yourself for things that you have not even done is unfair. In fact, it is because you constantly tell yourself that you are incapable. This leads to a lack of intellectual capability at that very moment.

Ask yourself, *Do things happen in life only because of you or do others contribute as well?* At the moment, you feel low about your *self* because, at some time, you have internalised that everything that is happening around you is happening only because of you.

So at this point, you feel that you are less than others, when in reality, you are not. This is actually your mind in the mode of self-rejection, and it is not you being less. Another important realisation to be made is that this inadequacy exists, *not because you are* inadequate but *because you think* that you are inadequate.

Each part of life until now is like a small puzzle that you have solved, and they are all needed to solve the complete puzzle. Every step was needed. At the surface of it all, you find the puzzle yet unsolved, and you give up, saying that you are less or inadequate. Instead, you need to tell yourself that you are very close now. In the next part, you will become capable of solving it.

Q: Why do we always think too much about our negatives and weaknesses?

A: This happens to most people who have *low self-esteem* or *low estimation of self.* It is like masochism—driving pleasure by inflicting pain on the *self.* Your mind considers the *self* a target, and it inflicts emotional pain by using self-rejecting thoughts. It's all in the mind, so the intensity of self-doubt increases when you think a bit too much about the ideal life, day in and day out, thinking about weaknesses, be they your incapabilities or your negative physical features or your negative personality traits.

Do you tell yourself statements such as "I am not good enough. I am a failure. I do not look good." Saying such things has never made anyone confident. Living a life with confidence is possible when you are not obsessively thinking about your weaknesses and negatives. Continually thinking about one's weaknesses and negative traits deviates people from their responsibilities and demands that need to be fulfilled. This eventually leads to lesser accomplishments, which in turn leads to the continuation of this vicious cycle of Self-negation.

Q: Why do others put me down?

A: This is another very common reason why people have low self-esteem. Most people are not assertive.

As a result, they end up allowing others to judge them and their lives. So if you do not stop these people in your life from commenting on your failures or weaknesses, you end up believing their statements and a sense of inadequacy about the *self* settles in. And then, instead of planning out your career, your life decisions, and tasks to enhance the *self*, you just get influenced by what others say to you, and eventually, you prove them right.

Even if you have planned on creating success, due to a lack of assertiveness, you end up believing the statements that others have said. This fails your planning. You have never been able to speak up for yourself, maybe because you do not trust your *self*. As long as you were a child, you looked up to others, and you trusted whatever they said about you. But now, things have changed. Now, you are not a kid anymore. Those who are confident and believe in their selves take steps despite all the odds. They know that listening to negative comments about their self is detrimental to their self-image.

Similarly, you also need to make a conscious effort to remain away and untouched by the negative judgements of people, even if these people are in your own circle, your own family, or work. This can be done by either staying away from such people or by assertively asking them to stop commenting about you. To be able to do this, you need to work on a few skills that you lack. This way, you will be able to get out from the state of self-doubt and self-rejection.

Q: Why does my mind connect everything to me?

A: Your mind is always busy trying to map some inadequacy or the other of the self as the reason for every failure. Your mind always has an ideal scenario as a benchmark for success. Your mind has to find some way or the other to hold itself responsible. The mind is in the 'all or nothing thinking' mode.

Those who do not have an idealistic life as the parameter of success, have no problem at all. And there are others like you, who are in strong clutches of the mind. The mind fails you by relating everything to some weakness of the self, even if that weakness is not a weakness in reality. Here the first step for you is to break this pattern of your mind. Only then, you can take the next step towards gaining self-confidence. This needs to be done systematically.

Q: Why am I not able to find solutions to my problems?

A: You want to change your self-image, but your struggle is that you are unable to discover the way. The first hurdle that exists in your mind is that it does not believe that you are good and that you have a meaningful existence. You will be able to connect the dots and create a positive self- esteem when you cross this hurdle.

Of course, it is hard to defeat the mind and motivate it to believe in the goodness of yourself. You have lived with a shallow sense of self for a long time, without knowing the Real You. But now, you have to turn it around.

Inner Self Integration is a wonderful technique that helps you to get there. Be committed to getting there. And once you are confident, you will be confident always.

Q: How important is a support system?

A: The word 'support system' itself talks about support. A support system is a group of people, including a circle of family and friends that are available to anyone for practical and emotional support. The mind believes whatever the people in your support system say.

In your case, either your close ones have not been there to tell you that you are good or they did not make you feel that you are really worthy. Maybe unknowingly, they have said a few negative things about you in the past which your mind has assimilated.

Those who have a good bond with the support system find it easy to live a life of confidence. It is recommended that you gain trust and courage to get in touch with family and friends who will always be there for you and think of doing good for you. They exist for everyone, so they exist for you as well.

Maybe until now, you were not open or aware that you need to connect to them. It is helpful to share what's in your heart with the ones who are there for your support. When you share your situation, they lend their support in some way or the other. Even if this support is in the form of a simple reassurance that you are good, it can do wonders for you.

After this, it becomes your responsibility to trust yourself. You should not talk to them about your weaknesses over and over again. Gain energy from them and grow it in your heart; and when you go back to them, tell that you are much better because of their help. When they see that their encouragement works, they will encourage you more.

Now, to conclude, you can say that until now, you felt low about yourself, more because of your thoughts and not because you are less. All this is a game played by the mind. Either you learn the way to get the mind in control or the mind will have control over your emotions. Sometimes, feeling less and inadequate is normal and happens to everyone in some situations. But when you know that you are experiencing a low because of the negative thinking cycle, it is important that you take charge of your mind and your thoughts.

Otherwise, your mind is capable of making things worse for you. Now that you have understood that it is about the thought patterns of your mind and not about your actual capability, you need to take voluntary action to change this involuntary functioning in the mind. It is definitely possible. If you have understood the actual reasons behind the low self- esteem correctly, you are ready to learn your next steps. It is a structured step-by-step process to create a positive self-esteem.

CHAPTER
Twenty Seven
Starting Afresh with Spiritual Energy

In the previous section, you learnt that all these years your low self-esteem was only because of the mind and not because you were incapable or less. You have learnt that it is the mind that was stuck, and you did not know how to deal with it. By continuing to be in the drift, you were giving away your power to the mind. And because of that, you remained in the same position all this while. At the same time, the fact is "What has happened till now, has happened." Now, you need to work on your mind. So get ready to rescue yourself.

Firstly, it is important to understand what confidence is. The word 'confidence' comes from the term 'confiding', which is related to the word 'fidelity.' Fidelity means being loyal. Here, 'confidence in self ' means 'being loyal to self.' Being confident is about 'confiding in the self.'

The next important aspect is to understand is "*Who is not loyal to the self and in what way?*"

The answer is "You!"

You are not loyal to yourself because you do not acknowledge and admire yourself. You are disloyal to your self because you remember only the negatives about your self. Now you need to do the reverse. Acknowledge the self for all the 'goodness' that is there in 'You' is a conscious task. You need to do this yourself. This way, you will have loyalty to your *self*. That is what confidence is. It is an act of having fidelity to self. This needs to be done throughout your life.

Secondly, even if you do not get the acknowledgement from others, you need to remember that you are good. You have to also remember that your goodness benefits others directly or indirectly. This is an effortless task that needs to come from within you. This effortless action will create a *positive self-image*, which means 'having a positive image of self.' This positive self- image is not dependent on anything outside.

You need to believe that your existence has a great value and significance. This significance also has to be perceived by your *self* first. Obviously, at the end of the day, this will create a great sense of trust in yourself.

The mind is a very important tool. You have to use this tool to create a set of positive thoughts about the *self*. You can live a life of self-respect and confidence only when you carry a set of positive thoughts in your mind, both at a conscious and subconscious level. These thought patterns have to be established deep in your subconscious mind.

Your mind may not be able to comprehend all this immediately because all the earlier thought patterns are hidden below your conscious awareness. Here, it becomes important for you to acknowledge those thoughts. Simultaneously, you need to identify new qualities about yourself. When you replace the negative thoughts with the newly identified qualities of your own self, you start gaining confidence. In the section of the book that follows, you will learn a step-by-step way to identify the qualities in you.

It does not matter whether you are an introvert or extrovert. You have a whole lot of capabilities and goodness in you that will help in building a positive self-esteem. To build a positive self-esteem, you need to allow yourself to explore the qualities and strengths within you. Make a commitment that you will always maintain an optimistic perspective no matter how absurd things are around you. Now onwards, you need to do a conscious task to feel better about your own self.

To live a life with a high self-esteem, you do not have to take yourself from rags to riches. It is about living a life with confidence in the self and having a sole agenda to create a sense of positivity around the self.

'Confidence' is not about the actual state of wealth or achievements alone. It is more about 'how you view your achievements.' Even a fairly well-off person can have a higher self-esteem compared to someone who has attained fortunes but still feels lower about the self. A person who lives a *self-fulfilled life* consciously chooses to craft a positive self-image by believing that he is good. He does not measure the level of success on the basis of quantity. Instead, to him, success is based on the satisfaction with the self, satisfaction with all the good that he has done. He derives this sense of satisfaction from within his own self, which in turn leads to quantitative results as well. All you need to have is faith in self.

Q: What are the ways to develop positive self-esteem?

A: Tell your mind, "**Life is what you create 'now', and not what has happened.**"

The mind has a habit of recollecting all the past events. And it misses out on the most important aspect—the present. The mind, like a 'pendulum in the clock', swings between two extremes—'the past' and 'the future.' In fact, it does not even stop. It keeps swinging 'left and right.' The present is something that the mind never sees.

You waste a lot of time thinking about all that has happened. Isn't it? It is funny that what has happened has happened and gone? The good part is that you still have access to *'the present moment.'*

This *present moment* is an opportunity to craft the future. The mind assesses the self-image on the basis of the past. It uses the assessment to find out the direction for the future. The mind is always occupied in planning the future. This way, it is busy assessing the past and imagining the future. Yet, there is a very important task that the mind does not remember—the execution of the plan.

This execution has to be done only in the present. In your situation, your mind has assessed its self as worthless and inadequate. The mind believes that you will not be able to create any success in the future. But now, you have to put an end to this pattern. To do this, commit to yourself that you will create confidence in your self by making the most of this present moment.

In the next few steps, you will learn how to do it.

Q: How do I connect with my *Inner Self* and find out my strengths?

A: This is an active task. Randomly list your strengths on a sheet of paper. These are some qualities that you or others appreciate about yourself. Your mind may rebel and say that there are no areas of strengths. However, this task has to be done consciously. List random things. It is important to believe that you are good and you have strengths. Tell your mind that at least ten such strengths exist. Keep writing. When you are done, read out all the strengths. These strengths can help you create huge success in anything that you do.

Remember that the **primary goal** is **confidence** and **positive self-esteem**. The **secondary goal** is to **accomplish things** as well. Accomplishments will become an evidence of your goodness and strengths. It is like one feeding the other in a cyclic form. Confidence leads to accomplishments and accomplishments lead to confidence. If you keep accomplishment as the primary objective of life, the confidence goes away. In such a case, your concept of success will be dependent on accomplishments, which may come and go. No accomplishment can stay forever, just like no tennis player can stay in the number one position always. No businessman can hold the top position all the time. However, one can always have confidence. You will have positive self-esteem if you keep yourself confident always.

When you are writing down your strengths, just believe that your *Inner Self* is aware of them. You need to stop all other thoughts that interfere. Trust that you will get to know about your strengths from within your *Inner Self.* It may be a hazy or abstract hint that your *Inner Self* will bring up to your conscious awareness. Just trust that hint. It can be anything. It may be your writing skills, your sense of humour, hard work, or loyalty to others. Even if it is the empathy that you feel for the needy, it is shown by your *Inner Self.* You have to actively believe that it is a strength.

The mind has a habit of comparing the achievements of the self with that of others. If you want to stop your mind from doing this, it needs to be motivated to think positively about the self. To do this, you need to actively identify positives in the self. Never think that your strengths are not as important as those of others. This is your journey, and it cannot be compared to any other person's journey. Everyone is in this world on a journey for a certain number of years. Each one has their unique strengths, as their journey demands. Similarly, you also have a set of strengths.

You need to use your strengths and make them great. It is your responsibility towards yourself to believe your strengths and create your own positive self-image. Trust your journey and accept that your journey is unique and has its own gestation period. As it is only you on your journey, you cannot compare your unique journey with anyone else. Your accomplishments need not be compared on the basis of time. It needs to be viewed as a journey. Positive self-esteem is about having a positive experience through this journey.

While writing your strengths, if you face difficulties, tell your mind that the words will come to you in some time. Keep your mind open. You will get hints about your strengths unexpectedly.

Q: How do I find the purpose of my life?

A: If you look at all the living or non-living objects around, you will realise that everything exists in this world to fulfil some purpose. Everything is caused. Everything is created for some purpose. Now, look at your hands. Nature has created this body in this world to fulfil some purpose. You need to forcefully make your mind believe that you too have been created for some unique purpose. This will help you in taking the next steps.

Q: How can I make myself better each day?

A: Another conscious task is to commit to your own self that you will improve your skills and capabilities. To accomplish this, you have to connect to your *Inner Self* and discover all the areas that you have to improve upon. Your *Inner Self* will give you a hazy idea about your areas of improvement, but *you* need to work on them. Make a commitment to yourself that you will improve in those areas in future. You need to actively craft your personality, skills, and capability. It could be adding educational qualifications, changing your wardrobe, your hairstyle, or joining guitar classes.

It is important to believe strongly and take the necessary action required to build a Positive Image. Commitment towards the Self can motivate you to take small steps towards effecting improvement. As you walk through this journey of improvement step-by-step, a day will come, when you start loving everything about yourself. As a result, it will show in your attitude and accomplishments. The world will also start appreciating you in the same manner. A person with positive self-esteem has no need for the world's acknowledgement. You need to be joyful and effortless in your action. This happens only when you know that you are good and you effortlessly make yourself better.

Q: How can I get rid of my negative thoughts?

A: You have been caught in the negative thought cycle for such a long time. As a result, it is normal that negative thoughts related to your past, impact you so often. Let it happen, it is normal. You should not expect the mind to think positive all the time. Everyone's mind thinks negatively very often. So from now on, whenever you experience negative thoughts of fear, self-doubt, doubts about whether you are doing the right thing or not, just be aware that it is happening in the moment.

Allow the negative thoughts and feelings to happen. When you have this awareness that it is happening to you, your mind will cease to pay attention to those thoughts. As a result, without going very deep into the negative thought cycle, your mind will come out of it very quickly. Avoid checking whether the mind is coming out or not. Your job is to allow the mind to complete the cycle. The moment mind gets free, bring your focus back on your goodness. Being loyal to the self is about confiding in the self.

An amazing sense of confidence is developed when each and every single step in the day is taken towards living the personal strengths. Get the best out of yourself and create small wins. Share these small wins with the people in your support system.

Request them to respect and motivate you. It is about the journey and not the destination.

When you remember your strengths and talent and when you start walking confidently, the journey of life gets you small and big accomplishments. These accomplishments add to your self-esteem at every mile that you arrive at. So do all that you can do. Create a new reality and be open to receive pleasant surprises from this journey.

PART
Seven

Ending Fear

CHAPTER
Twenty Eight
Knowing the Fear

It is true that the symptoms that you have as of now exist. But there is not a single person who is NOT surrounded with challenges. A question arises— "*Why is this fear happening to you?*"

Your answer to this will be, "I do not know."

In reality, there are few fears that may be known to you. But you may not know many others.

The truth is that the situation you are in now is actually passive, but your mind perceives the fear of the future, which is the source of this fear. This fear of the future is based on some deep thoughts that are stored in your subconscious mind. This does not mean that if someone else is in a similar situation, he or she will not feel anxious. But surely, the intensity will depend on the way the mind thinks. It has to do with how your mind imagines the future.

Have you noticed that some people imagine their future as all negative, whereas others see future as a challenge or a game that they can win? What goes differently for these two sets of people? Now another question that arises is, "Why do you feel so impacted?"

Indeed you have a lot of negative thoughts about the future. So there will be an impact. But why does it impact you and why this much? The answer is—the mind. Yes, it is the mind that makes it all difficult for you. The mind indulges in continuous negative thinking that makes you feel anxious.

The next question that may occur to your mind is—*"Are we not supposed to think about the future when we know that it has an impact on us?"*

The answer is NO.

It is true, that as of now, you cannot stop thinking. And this thinking is your disease. The word Disease, as you know, is *'Dis Ease'*, which means 'Not in Ease.' When you think at a subconscious level, all the thoughts of fear manifest in the form of fear. The funny thing is that despite knowing that nobody can predict the future, your mind still thinks continuously. What is funnier is that you do not even know that you think this way.

Nobody knows how to 'not think about the future.' Surely, some people know how to distract the mind. But it does not work for too long. Does it? You need some awareness to get out of the mind's trap. Thinking is aimed at trying to change the future. The future will happen on its own but because you imagine it, you get fearful. Being fearful and doubtful leads to a 'reaction' in your body. This reaction is called 'fear.' This means that if you stop being fearful and doubtful, your life will change.

Let us understand the **Reason Behind Fear**. If symptoms of fear exist, it is certain that there must be some subconscious fear behind it. It may seem to you that you have no fear. But nothing happens in this world without a reason. Your fears may be suppressed in your subconscious awareness. But they exist. Let us now get to know all the reasons behind fear, and then, you will find it very easy to find your way out.

Q: Why do I feel anxious and nervous all the time?

A: Different people have either of the following reasons that lead to fear. Some people even have a mix of these reasons.

REASONS FOR FEAR

1. **The Challenging Situation**

   Occasional feeling fearful is a normal part of everyday life, even when nothing major is likely to happen in the future. But when there is a situation that is really challenging, anyone can get impacted.

   Fear is an indication that the mind is severely impacted by some fearful thoughts about the future. These thoughts are related to anticipated demands and pressures that are likely to happen in the future.

   A minimal level of fear is needed for a person to remain connected to the motive. But when the level of fear increases and crosses a limit, then it begins to impact the functionality of the person.

   A few situations that can make anyone experience fear are constant deadlines, overcrowded working conditions, short-term illness, travelling in an unfamiliar city, beginning a new job or project, concern about health, weight, fitness, concerns regarding money, wasting time, being lonely, etc.

Fear can happen because of such situations. But it is important to find the way out. You cannot continue to think about the future negatively because of a certain situation and 'not do' anything about it. Fear is a response of the body that indicates that you have to work on the situation, instead of being afraid.

2. **Lack of a Support System**

The word "support system" itself talks about support. A support system is the group of people from one's family or circle of friends that is available to a person for practical or emotional support. The mind believes whatever the people in the support system say. Whether the situation is big or small, people feel afraid when they lack a support system. Those who have a strong support system find it easy to deal with challenging situations because they connect with their support system on time.

However, those who are alone and do not have any sound support system find it very difficult to deal with any normal situation. They feel more anxious compared to those who have a good support system. Sometimes people in the support system do not speak in the ideal way that you expect, but that does not mean that the support system is not there, or they do not intend you good. Sometimes, in their heart, they believe that you are good, but because they are very protective of you, they end up cautioning you, which appears negative to you.

It is recommended that you gain trust and courage to get in touch with family and friends who will always be there for you and who always think for your good. Everyone has them, and you do too. Maybe until now, you were not open and aware that you need to connect to them. It helps to just share your feelings with the ones who are there for you. When you share your feelings and your situation, they definitely lend their support in some way or the other. Even if this support is in the form of some simple reassurance, it can do wonders for you.

3. **The Lack of a Coping Behaviour**

   Sometimes, people do not know how to deal with a particular situation. This becomes the reason for their fear. So it is more about how to deal with the situation and not about the future. If one works on the present with conviction, the future will definitely be good. To cope means to contend with difficulties, to act, and to overcome them. This is an ability that not everyone possesses. There are solutions to every problem, but not everyone knows this. Most people start thinking about the adverse circumstances that may happen in the future.

Everyone can find a solution to every problem. There are no solutions to **facts**. Traffic on the road is a fact. But not being able to reach is a **problem** that can be solved. Fear will surely occur if you allow your mind to get into the rut of cyclically thinking about the consequences of being late. Similarly, you need to identify the problem associated with your situation. Your mind thinks so rigorously that you find it really difficult to disassociate the fact from the problem. So if you want to remove fear, you need to develop a sound coping behaviour to deal with the situation, and thereby, assure a positive future.

4. **The Temperament**

   Temperament is the way one thinks, behaves, or reacts. It is a distinguishing psychological characteristic of any person. These characteristics are formed because of various factors such as childhood experiences, learning, and genetic makeup. Sometimes, the situation is not too big or complex, but the temperament of the person leads to fear. Most people think that having an optimistic temperament works and having a pessimistic temperament leads to fear.

However, there is another reality. People end up feeling anxious, because of some temperament like perfectionism, agreeableness, or even friendliness. It is true that one cannot create or expect perfection in all conditions. One cannot be agreeable in all situations. And not in all situations can one be friendly. Such temperament leads to fear of the future and this way, one ends up having fear. So it becomes important to understand your temperament.

When you trust yourself and start focussing on taking the right actions, there will be no fear. So if you want to live happily and peacefully, it is important to know and accept your *self*. Your current situation may indeed be difficult for you, but at the same time, it is very important for you to first develop the needed calmness and composure within yourself. With a calm mind, you will be able to think straight and become capable of seeing the future clearly.

In such a situation, people experience a lot of emotions like self-doubt, fear of the future or helplessness. So you need to first deal with these emotions within yourself. And then, you can decide the way forward. In the second part of the book, you will be able to create a future full of peace.

Q: How can one be self-confident?

A: Anyone may feel anxious if he or she is in a similar situation as you are in. But because this situation has happened all of a sudden, you feel clueless. This feeling of cluelessness is normal at the moment because until now, everything seemed to be going well for you. You can be clueless about the solution to the situation. But this must not continue for too long. You must connect to family or friends to learn how to get out of the situation. If it is something that you need professional advice for, go ahead. Whatever it may take, emerge out of this cluelessness.

Q: How Can I Feel Secure?

A: Fear has happened to you because you never concentrated on your *self*. Your mind is constantly thinking about the plans and the tasks to be done, without any belief in self. You are either overly critical of yourself or doubtful of yourself. And all this while, your mind has been busy worrying so much about the future. In fact, this is one of the most important reasons that has led to fear. You never knew that you needed to focus on your abilities instead of giving power to negative thoughts about future. And now, the body has been forced bring the concentration to your *self*.

CHAPTER
Twenty Nine
Discovering Eternal Peace in All Moments

What has happened till now has happened. Now, you need to work on your mind.

If you understand and implement the following steps genuinely, you will be able to move on from this fear, which is nothing but a manifestation of a negative thought cycle. For a few moments, the mind needs to be kept silent.

What you receive now has to be forced into the mind. Of course, the mind will rebel, it will object. But your task is to just focus and understand everything that is told from now onwards.

You will see that almost all doubts get addressed on their own. If you genuinely help, you will be able to understand the action that needs to be done. When the action required is performed, it will lead to harmony and balance. This is all that you aspire for. Isn't it?

So help yourself to understand and internalise all that will be shared with you in a few moments from now.

Let us begin.

Today's life is fast-paced and very competitive. Everyone is under a lot of pressure to get approval. But when this pressure turns into fear, the problem begins. Even medical Science recommends on working on one's lifestyle if one wants to get rid of fear. If you need medical treatment for fear, it is recommended to seek it. Yet along with medication, you need to work on your thoughts and on your life. At the same time, fear cannot be just eliminated by willpower. But if you understand a few basics, you can see the results right away.

What is Fear?

Fear refers to being worried and tensed because of possible misfortune or danger. Fear is about choking. So in your case, "Who is choking you?" It is interesting to learn that "Your mind is choking you." Subconsciously, your own mind carries thoughts of fear of the unknown future, which lead to this physiological manifestation called fear. These thought patterns run deep down in your subconscious mind, and they emerge in the form of bodily response. Fear is a normal corrective mechanism of the body. Its goal is to stop these thoughts or perhaps to stop your mind. In other words, it is a survival mechanism of the body that comes from the theory of fight-or-flight.

When any animal faces a probable threat, its body prepares itself for fight- or-flight so that it can deal with the threat. It is similar in your case as well. Your mind is aware of the probable threat in the future. The body prepares itself by making the heart beat faster and breathe lesser, such that you can either run away or fight against the threatening situation.

A few thoughts of fear that may run in your mind may include—

"I have to do this otherwise..."

"I cannot afford to waste any more time; if I do..."

"I have no choice but to..."

Does your mind not repeat such statements all the time?

These thoughts create a sense of fear in you when the truth is that life happens on its own. Your job is to just continue putting in your efforts and playing your role. At the same time, there are other factors, as well, that are responsible for any consequence in the future. You may not be able to comprehend all this as of now because all these patterns are below your conscious awareness. The bodily symptoms of fear are the indications that you are not doing something you are supposed to.

When animals encounter any threatening situation, fear becomes a motivating factor for them. They either run very fast or fight hard with the enemy. They do not take fear to the mind because they do not think, they simply act. Since we have a mind, we need to first sort the mind and then, we can act. At the conscious level, you may not be aware of any fear that you have. Your mind may say, *"I am capable of dealing with every challenge, and I have always been doing this."* But subconsciously, these symptoms tell that there is fear.

Q: How can I live a life free of fear?

A: It is good that these symptoms of fear are manifesting externally. Because now, you know that you need to work on the cause. If this is happening to you, you need to know that the mind is sending you a signal that something needs to be done, both at the mind level and also in the real world.

1. The first level of work has to be done within the mind. The first step is to **accept that fear can happen.** Stop amplifying thoughts like, "*I had never imagined this happening to me, what has happened is the worst.*" These kinds of thoughts will make your mind feel even more anxious. The manifestation of fear is normal. But consciously over- living this fear increases its intensity.

2. The next step is to **identify what is causing you to feel pressurised**. This is a very important thing that you need do by going deep into the subconscious mind and identifying the fear. Even if your mind is reasoning a certain way, identifying and accepting the fear is the only solution. Everyone has fears but working on the fear is important.

The future is unknown; however, at the same time, it is certain that you have the present in your hands. There are parts of the future that your action in the present can certainly impact. You should not think about the parts that are not in your control.

Q: Is it okay to disconnect from the situation or people?

A: The mind is smart enough to pick up cues and take you back into the thought patterns. So the minute anything related to thoughts of the future appears in front of you, your mind takes it as a cue. Taking it out of your sight is taking it out of your mind. Of course, you cannot take everything out of sight. But whatever best you can do, you must.

If the fear is because of a particular person, tell him or her that you are experiencing a difficulty at the moment and that you need some time for yourself, and tell them that you will be back in a few moments. Walk away during that time. Cool down and try to discover the actual trigger point of fear. Fear is an impact of a trigger inside the subconscious mind and not outside. During your time off, you need to identify the thoughts of fear that arise because of the trigger. You need to practice this because the cycle of fear works very fast.

Q: How can we identify the triggers that induce fear?

A: The mind makes you feel anxious because of some triggers. Think for a while—try to determine what appears in front of you, taking your mind back into that cycle of subconscious thinking, and making you anxious. Understanding the triggers is crucial. Knowing the trigger will help you find the solution to this pattern. When you are aware of the trigger, see what best you can do towards working on that trigger.

Also, the moment the trigger happens, be prepared, that now that the trigger is here, it is possible the mind may go back into the cycle of fear. You need to tell yourself at that moment, "Now when this trigger is here, it is normal for me to feel anxious." Awareness of the pattern and the trigger is a big achievement. Slowly, with a few days of practice, you will see that the mind loses its association of the trigger and the related feeling. If you continue this way, very soon, the fear will cease, despite the presence of the trigger.

Q: How Do We Create Living?

A: Now, when you are aware of the reasons and triggers behind the fear, you need to actively work on them. You have to consciously tell yourself that you have to work on those ignored areas of your life. Your mind may deny it and find it really difficult, but taking one step at a time will surely help you reach success.

Do not burden yourself with the thought, "*Now that you have complete awareness of fear, it should go away.*" Such an expectation will only add to the fear. So at the moment, when you experience the symptoms of fear, just be aware that it is happening, and allow it to happen.

The moment you are aware that it is happening to you, your mind will complete the cycle of fear and come out of it, instead of going deep. You do not have to check whether the mind is coming out of it or not. Your job is to take the corrective action and allow the mind to change its pattern gradually. It is more important to shift focus to the steps that have to be taken during the day. This will help you create a new way of living. Move in this direction, and create your small wins. If you have people in your support system, request them to acknowledge your efforts. This is an active task that needs to be done at the time the fear is present.

You need to replace the negative thoughts about the future that constantly run in your mind. You need to trust yourself and your capability. Fear happens because you allow your mind to be afraid of the future. Once you trust yourself and focus on your actions, your mind will also believe that the future will be positive.

To do this, you need to create a new statement about the future. This new statement will give you peace. Take a few moments to write your new statement. Do not think you will be able to turn everything around right away. But writing this new statement is your first step, surely.

Your statement can be "*I am putting in my best efforts, and this will definitely lead to a positive future.*" It may take some time for a complete change to happen. But every time, you say this statement, it will give you relief. Your genuine steps, commitment, trust in self and proactive effort will definitely bring the change.

Change is possible only if you can remind yourself of the new statement the minute you feel anxious. The more you practice, the more this new view of yourself will become a normal response of your mind. The mind is a very sharp system that can be trained. This way, new layers of memory will form over the old memory about yourself and your capability. A day will come when you will no longer remember the old thoughts.

Feel good that you have learnt to sense the triggers and create a new view of life and yourself. It is this change in you that will bring about a change in the mind. You need to remember, that you do not have to measure the change. Bring the change, do not measure it. One day, the change will happen, and there will be no fear.

Fear-Relaxation Exercise

To help you be in harmony with yourself and the situation, let us learn a fear- relaxation exercise. This helps in eliminating fear instantaneously. It is called "Watch the Breath" exercise.

You can do this exercise either lying down on a mattress, on the ground, or sitting in a comfortable chair. It is important to ensure that the body is comfortable.

1. **First Step:**

   Close your eyes. Let go of your control over the body, as if it does exist. Let your arms, legs, and the whole body be very loose as if you are allowing all the weight of the body to drop into the earth.

2. **Second Step:**

   Now try to absorb the feeling that you are not this body. The body is as neutral as the chair or the ground below. Now note that this body is breathing on its own. Bring your attention to your nose. Feel the air coming in through your nostrils and feel it going out. This is all happening on its own. Your job is to just feel it.

3. **Third Step:**

   Feel your breath. Feel the air coming in and going out. Let the air come in and go out on its own. Breath is the easiest tool you can use to calm yourself, and it is available to you all the time. The breath also happens on its own, like a river that flows by itself. Just feel this flow of air coming in and going out.

   During this exercise, your mind may wander. It may think. Some random thoughts may occur. Let them come. The moment you realise they are coming, bring your focus back to the flow of the air that is coming in and going out.

4. **Fourth Step:**

   Now with every breath that is coming in, experience all the positivity of this universe coming inside you; and with the breath that goes out, feel all the fear and discomfort of your body going out. Positivity is coming in, and all the fear is going out. You are just an observer. You are not the body and not even this breath. Now feel the calmness in the whole body. Experience this calmness in every part of the body.

5. **Fifth Step:**

   Now, slowly, very slowly, open your eyes. Experience this calmness even with open eyes. Feel your breath, it is so calm. And feel your mind which is also so light. It has no thoughts as of now. Feel the calmness and composure. You need to experience your existence, even with your eyes open. If you can create the calmness by connecting to yourself now, you can do this all the time.

Now congratulate yourself on having witnessed the effect of this exercise. Very soon, a day will come, when this calmness becomes a natural reflex of your body. With practice, you will need only a few seconds to create the same calmness even in the middle of a challenging situation.

PART *Eight*

Goodbye to A Depressed Life

CHAPTER *Thirty*

Understanding the Deprivation

It is true that the situation that you are in as of now exists. But do you know that there is not even one person, who is NOT surrounded by situations? It is a different fact though, that the situation any given person is surrounded with may not be the same as those experienced by the other. Furthermore, the impact of the situation appears big only to that person who experiences it. Nobody else can feel that impact, exactly the way the experiencer experiences. It is likewise in your case as well.

Another question that arises is that *"When all the situations are happening around you and not inside you, why are you sad?"*

Your answer to this will be, *"I feel sad inside because all this is happening around me."*

It is important to know that in between these two incidents—the situation and your feeling—there is a subtle gap that the mind doesn't understand. The situations that exist around you are actually passive and happen passively, but your mind perceives the situation as good or bad because of some conditioning. You feel the impact of the situation according to that conditioning. This does not mean that if someone has experienced some loss, he or she will not feel sad.

But surely, the intensity of the feeling will depend on the conditioning of the mind. It is about how your mind perceives the situation. Have you noticed that some people see something as an obstacle, whereas others see the same thing as a challenge—a game? What goes differently? The impact is experienced only by your mind in a particular manner, and that's what makes it more traumatic for you. Now another question that arises is, "Why do you feel so impacted?" Indeed if the situation exists, there will be an impact. But why to you, and why this much? The answer is—the mind. It is the mind that makes it all different for you. The mind indulges in continuous thinking and makes you feel sad.

The next question that may come to your mind is—"*Are we not supposed to think if something happens and impacts us?*"

The answer is NO.

It is true that as of now, you cannot stop thinking. Thinking is your *dis- ease.* As stated earlier, constant thinking only turns the mind into a madhouse. The funny part is that despite thinking so much, you still remain where you are or worse. In this process of thinking, you waste a lot of time—your active life. Nobody knows how to *not think.*

Surely, some people know how to distract the mind, but it does not work for too long. So you need some awareness to get out of the mind's trap. The world has misery because people think. Thinking is an attempt at changing, which leads to reaction. The situation in itself is always neutral, but how the experiencer perceives it makes all the difference. Perceiving and thinking lead the reaction. This means that if perceiving and thinking changes, your world can change.

Let us understand the reason behind this emotion of sadness and helplessness. If the emotion has existed, it is certain that there is some reason behind it. It may seem to you that there is no reason for your sadness, but nothing happens in this world without a reason. The reason may be suppressed in your subconscious awareness, but it exists. Let us learn all the reasons behind your sadness, and then, you will find it very easy to create a way out.

Q: How much impact does a situation have on the mind?

A: Feeling sad is a normal part of everyday life, even when nothing major has happened. But when a severe situation happens, it is obvious that anyone would be affected. A few situations that can make anyone sad are trauma, grief, financial troubles, career problems, wrong concepts about the self, a sudden increase in responsibility, major issues in marriage, issues with personal relationships, divorce and separation, issues with children, the death of a loved one, etc. Any of these situations can lead to sadness. It is normal.

However, it is important to first go through the emotion and then do something about it. Of course, there are no solutions to some situations. But there are solutions to many problems. For example, the death of a close one or a breakup in a relationship are situations that have no solution, and they will lead to grief—it is normal.

But the problem that arises because of these situations is the difficulty in moving on. One can definitely find a solution to this problem. Problems are like puzzles that need to be solved. And if a puzzle exists, the solution definitely exists. Therefore, the first step is to distinguish between the situation and the problem.

Q: Does the sadness increase if one does not have a support system?

A: The word "support system" itself talks about support. Whether the situation is big or small, people feel sad if they lack a support system. Those who have a strong support system find it easy to deal with challenging situations because they connect with their support system on time, whereas those who are alone and do not have a sound support system find it very difficult to deal with any normal situation. They feel sadder compared to those who have a good support system.

Q: What is the way to get rid of feelings of guilt?

A: Guilt is a common emotion that people experience along with sadness. As it is not a pleasant situation at the moment, you are clueless about why it happened, and your mind is busy evaluating your own self. This happens because the mind has a tendency to wind and rewind the movie of your life. It looks out for reasons to put the blame on you.

As a result, you often think you must have messed up somewhere, and that's why all of this is happening. The occurrence of this thought is natural to anyone who is in such a situation. It is normal.

For now, the first step for you is to stop blaming yourself and stop feeling guilty. To do this, you can say to yourself, *"If I could do something different, I would; but because I couldn't, so I didn't."* Isn't it true? Yes, it's very simple. Saying this a number of times will help you come out of guilt.

Q: How can one deal with a sense of emptiness?

A: Emptiness is an emotion that arises when you are in the middle of a situation. It's something that needs to be understood well. Emptiness or numbness is the **absence of emotion**. The feeling of emptiness is a corrective mechanism of the mind to deal with the situation of shock. In some way, it actually protects the mind. However, if it continues for a long time, you must work on understanding the numbness. Emptiness gives the mind some time to accept the trauma and resolve it inside. Normally, it goes away after some time. But if it does not, seeking professional help is recommended.

Q: What is the way to handle shock?

A: The third emotion that people usually experience with sadness is shock. You are in a state of sadness because you didn't expect this situation. You ask yourself how you didn't know this earlier. You are so used to a predictable life with happy things and happy situations that you never imagined that this situation could happen. So in truth, it is not about the current situation, it is about the unexpectedness and unpredictability of life. Whereas there is another reality, that nothing is sudden. What you are experiencing today is a consequence of several things that have already happened in the past.

Q: How does one deal with helplessness?

A: Anyone would feel sad if he or she were in a similar situation that you are in. But because this situation has happened suddenly, you may feel helpless. This feeling of helplessness is normal at the moment because until now everything seemed to be going well for you. But if it continues for too long, something is not right. You can be clueless about the solution to the situation, but this must not continue for too long. You must connect to family or friends and learn how to get out of this situation. If it is something that you need professional advice for, go ahead. But emerge out of this helplessness.

Memorising the Past

You are sad not because of what has happened, but more because there are memories of the past.

It hurts because your mind constantly thinks about the good timesof the past.

It is similar to a case where you visit a dentist and he pulls out a decayed tooth. Even after a month, your tongue runs over it continuously because, at a subconscious level, your mind misses the tooth there. This is an involuntary action of the mind. Similarly, even when you know at a logical level that the situation would have happened anyway because there were reasons, it is the mind that memorises and creates the pain. This is normal and happens to all.

As the information in the memory cannot be erased, there is only one solution that one can work on. You need to create new layers of memory. This means that only when you start viewing the same situation in a new light, your mind will become silent. This way, you will see the same situation with a new perspective, and your mind will memorise new positive information. This needs to be practised. You need to make your mind register new layers of memory every time thoughts of the past appear.

CHAPTER
Thirty One

Liberation from Self-Destruction & Living Happily

It is the mind that gets stuck, and you do not know how to deal with it. By continuing to be in the drift, you were giving away your power to the mind. And because of that, you remained in the same position all this while. Remember this—"What has happened till now, has happened." Now, you need to work on your mind.

To know the way to create happiness, you need to learn two things - happiness and unhappiness.

The word 'happiness' comes from the word 'happening.' So those are who are with 'the happening' are happy. This also means that those who are not with 'the happening' will be unhappy.

If you stay away from unhappiness, you will easily come into the state of happiness. Unhappiness is a state where your mind is not with 'the happening.' It means that your mind wants to change the situation. This need to change the situation is like a game that happens in the mind.

This game has two sources of unhappiness - *I want...* and *I don't want...*

The Game of Want

Let us now understand the first source of unhappiness - "I want..."

This is a game that happens in your mind all the time. The mind wants something more, something better. Perhaps the most important fact is that it 'wants something.' You experience sadness because your mind wants something. As the mind wants, you start putting in efforts to attain the things the mind wants. It can be a desired object or a desired situation that you want to be in.

There are **four outcomes** of this game of want.

1. Firstly, this wanting a particular thing or a situation generates a feeling of stress and fear in you.
2. Secondly, while the mind is playing its game of 'want', when you act in a particular direction but you still do not get the desired result or the object, frustration and sadness result. Simply speaking, despite your best efforts, when you do not get what you want, you feel sad.
3. Thirdly, despite your efforts, if the result is slightly different from how your mind wanted it to be, you will experience a greater sense of sadness. You feel frustrated, thinking about how you missed it so closely. This also makes you feel sad.
4. The fourth outcome is the funniest. If you get what your mind wanted, a new want is born because now you are convinced that it is because of your efforts that the results happened, whereas your efforts are just a part of the game. Efforts definitely contribute, but there are so many other things as

well, that are responsible for that result. So if you get what you want, you get into the illusion that it is only because of you that results happen.

This way a new game starts which brings you to the four probable outcomes once again, i.e., three probabilities of feeling sad and one chance of putting the self in this 'game of wanting' once again. Isn't that funny? Ultimately, it is the same outcome—sadness. It doesn't matter which category you lie in, you need to end this game of wanting in your mind. This certainly does not mean that you should stop wanting anything, stop going to work, or stop going to the grocery store.

Want is about "desiring greatly or wishing for", whereas *need* is about "being in the necessity of." This word 'necessity' is the differentiator here.

Your first step is to **observe the difference between what you need and what you want**. This way, your mind starts thinking in a new direction. So please be prepared for a lot of resistance from the mind.

Ask yourself, *"Isn't this unhappiness present because of some scarcity in the mind?", "Isn't this feeling of scarcity (and thereby pain), a choice that you have made unconsciously?"*

Yes, you definitely have the choice to suffer or not. It can also be called 'neediness.' This neediness is the ultimate source of sadness. But for now, you have to observe this habitual sense of neediness in your mind. Understanding this new concept is an active task.

The Game of "I Don't Want"

The second source of unhappiness is **I don't want…**

Interestingly, there is another pain game of the mind—'The Don't Want.' These days, you very often hear yourself saying, "I don't want this…", "I don't want that…" so much that you even make a declaration of the future by saying "I can never take this…", I will never let that happen…", "I will never do this…" and so on. This is called **aversion**.

Aversion is 'not liking something' or 'wanting to get rid of something.' Your mind carries aversion towards a lot of things. This leads to suffering, especially during the times you encounter those specific situations, people, or things. Aversion is another game similar to that of scarcity.

The mind plays this game of aversion and makes you sad. Nobody can remain happy in the situation that you are in now. But you still have a choice to suffer or not to. You can exercise this choice by remembering the fact that you have a choice.

The moment you encounter the situation or the person that your mind is averse to, tell your *self*—

"This situation is, this situation is, this situation is, this situation is, but I am also, and I have a choice to be peaceful, I choose to be peaceful."

By saying this, you will be able to distinguish between the incident and your choice.

This does not mean that you should not do anything about the situations. But do you know that you become sad only in the situations that your mind thinks are unavoidable? By saying the above lines, you will come to accept the situation, and you will be able to choose peace in the middle of the situation.

Also, note that you experience sadness mainly because of your wanting something. So 'not wanting something' is also 'wanting something else.' Understand the difference between what you need and what you want. As explained earlier, want is about 'desiring greatly' or 'wishing for' while **need** is about "being under the necessity of."

All that is necessary will keep on happening on its own. Nobody can stop what is necessary. Nature ensures that what is necessary is done. But the moment your mind wants to change something, you become sad for no reason. It can also be said that you become sad 'unnecessarily.'

Your next question must be – "How to not want?"

To not want, you simply need to do what is necessary and not what your mind wants or wishes for. This calls for creating a distinction between the mind and you. When you allow life to move on its own, you do not get caught in the trap of the mind.

Q: Should we allow the mind to think negative thoughts?

A: It is well said that "Whatever is observed will get controlled."

The same way, when you observe your mind, you are out of the game of the mind. It is actually that simple. You need to make this a new way of life if you want to live in peace. So the next time you are feeling sad, observe that your mind is playing with a thought. Doing this, you will realise that the thought is either about wanting something or not wanting something.

Observe the 'neediness' in your mind. You cannot stop the mind from playing this game. But you can create a subtle difference if you practice observing your own mind. The difference will be that, over time, you will start relishing the activity of the mind. You need to deal with the mind like how one deals with a baby.

The baby will throw tantrums in the form of thoughts about its 'wants.' Do not ignore the baby. Also, do not serve the baby, by giving in into its crying. Just watch and know that the baby is cranky at the moment. After some time, you will find the baby becomes okay. Obviously, the baby will not be happy with you, because you did not fulfil its demand. But you will see that the sadness goes away slowly.

This way, you will develop an ability to see the game of the mind, and then, the mind will get disciplined. You will find moments of peace occurring intermittently. With practice, a day will come when things will be the other way round. Your life will have several moments of peace, with very few dips of sadness. A few moments of sadness are a part of everybody's life. It is normal.

Q: How can I make my life useful?

A: This may appear impossible. Now listen to your mind. Your mind must be saying "*What is the point of living this life?*" The truth is a little different. Go back to the days when you were young. There were many unfavourable and unexpected incidents. They happened despite your best efforts, and you do not even remember them today. Indeed, many have happened and gone. This present situation also has happened and it will go. It is only your mind that is still giving reality and continuity to the situation.

Your mind attempts to present it as your failure and continues living this sense of failure in the present. This becomes a blockage for you to see the right and do the right.

Whenever your mind asks a question - "*How can I get out of this sense of uselessness?*" ask your *self* a question - "*Who told me that my life is useless?*"

Then answer to your *self* – *"Nobody."*

Now ask again, *"Then what can I do to feel better?"*

Then answer, *"I am already free to feel better."*

Talking to one's own *self* a number of times will reduce the mind's compulsive thinking. See how many people are benefitted from you directly or indirectly. There are many people who need you. Your life is useful to so many people. This is a conscious task that you need to perform in your mind. When you are able to count those people, call them or go and meet them. This will make you feel better.

Q: How can we shift the focus from negative thinking to seeing the good that exists in the present moment?

A: This is a conscious task. If you think about the good in the present, there is no way the past can bother you. Tell yourself, *"I am a genuine person. And because I am a genuine person, there are so many good things that exist around me."* By saying this in your mind, you will create a positive feeling once again.

While saying this, you need to force your own mind to think about the good things that exist. If you think voluntarily, you will get to know about them. This will make you feel abundant. A person who lives in abundance doesn't want anything. Either there is abundance or scarcity. Whatever you focus on grows. Similarly, if you start focussing on abundance, your eyes will see a lot of good things that already exist in abundance around you.

Q: Is it okay if the mind goes in bouts of negative spiral thinking?

A: Even if you are aware of the steps that are needed to create happiness, your mind may not be able to fully get rid of thinking in circles. It is normal. If you start working on the steps that are taught, you will be able to create a few spaces where there is peace and freedom. Yet these moments may not be like a straight line. Whenever your mind goes back in the bouts of thinking, allow it to do so. Doing so, you will create some peace. This is a great position, to begin with.

Q: How can one do the right thing?

A: If you know what needs to be done, there is a chance that you may find difficulty in implementing it. This is normal. It happens to those who experience a continued phase of feeling low. Let us understand the reason behind the difficulty. Your mind may be thinking—if you are experiencing so much sadness, how can you take action? But the truth is that all actions happen on their own. You are not the doer of anything. Actions happen with respect to the prevailing situations.

Now in your case, your action will be a response to the situation. If you allow the righteous action to happen, you will feel at ease; but if you resist, you will add to your sadness. Tell yourself, *"I am not the doer of this; it has to happen through me. I allow it the right to happen through me."* Saying this a number of times in your mind, you will be able to perform your righteous action with ease. This way, you will be able to create happiness for yourself. Now allow yourself to go ahead in that direction.

The mind may rebel, reject, and go back to incidents from the past because it wants to remain sad. Refrain from going down that negative route. It will not fetch anything, it will make you passive instead, and again, this will kill the scope of creating a happy life. It's like this scenario—if your closed one has slipped and fallen into a ditch and is asking for help, what would you do? Would you keep criticising and cursing him or her at the time, or would you get him or her out? This close one is you. So decide.

Q: How do we create a new world for ourselves?

A: This step is only possible when you are done with the emotional bit. Slowly but certainly, you need to create your own new world and your own new life where the past is not allowed to drop in. Take the opportunity to try something new that you never thought you would do. Everyone moves on, and so should you.

Remember...the purest form of happiness is hidden in your own self. This is the time for realisation and commitment to the self. Loving yourself can happen by doing the small things that you love doing. It may be going for a bike ride, going for a new haircut, calling and meeting old friends, anything of the like. Remember that happiness is all about believing that a better place exists for you now.

To conclude, here are a few statements that you can say to your own self. This will serve as a quick recap of all the learning. You can say these lines in your mind to fortify the concept in a very simple way. These are very simple affirmations that can be really useful and can be practised daily. So repeat these lines in your mind.

Say in your mind—

1. **"This Grief Was Good for Me."**

   I repeat – "This Grief was good for me."

   It was a process that you needed to realise that you have to always take care of your own Self. You needed to learn to give yourself priority over anything else. You need to live this life the way it moves, but not lose touch with your *self*. It is important to depend on the Self for happiness. You need to feel good within your *self*. This is a tough process, but still, every passing moment is healing you and bringing you out of the grieving state. You are learning to depend on your own self for all the happiness that you need.

2. The next statement that you have to say to yourself is—

   "I am lucky to have this brand new life once again."

   I repeat – "I am lucky to have this brand new life once again."

   The life that you have lived till now is not a reality anymore. It has happened and gone. Today, life offers you freedom once again to turn everything around. You get another chance because you are genuine. If you weren't, you would still be continuing that sad life. And it's a new life, where you have your best friend who needs you. This best friend is your *self*. Be with your *self* and stand beside yourself.

3. That last statement that you have to say to yourself is—

   "I Live Life."

   I repeat – I Live Life.

Learn to trust again. Live life, and never let a bad experience keep you from living your life to the fullest.

- To do this, close your eyes, and keep your body still. Now with your eyes closed, experience your existence inside this inner world. The blank space that you see is your Self. This is not your body but your own *self.*
- Tell yourself—*"I am", "I am", "I am..."*
- Now, slowly open your eyes and look all around.
- Now say, "*This world is, This world is, This world is, This world is, and I Am.*"
- Now close your eyes once again and experience your existence. Say *"I am", "I am", "I am."*
- Now open your eyes once again and say, *"I am and the world is."*
- Now with open eyes, experience your existence, and experience the calmness in your system. This is being happy.

Live Happy, Live Full, Life is Beautiful.

PART *Nine*

Mind Control Technique to Handle Anger

CHAPTER
Thirty Two
Knowing Anger

First of all, you need to what anger is and what is happening to you. When you know that exactly, the later part of the course will help you learn a step- by-step way to deal with reasons behind the anger.

So let us first understand—**What is Anger?**

Anger is an emotion that you feel. It would be better to say that anger happens to you. Remember the last time you experienced anger.

How would you describe your situation? You would probably say, *"I got angry."*

Anger is a normal emotion that can happen to anyone who gets frustrated when something that is desired doesn't happen or when something undesired continues for a long time.

Now, you have understood that being angry is bad and that one should not get angry. You have learnt that anger "comes." You experience anger, and you say *"I am getting angry."* Dealing with this natural emotion is futile. It is more important to learn that anger is a secondary emotion that is a consequence of the primary emotions of frustration and fear. In simple words, this means that first, there is a fear of future. If it continues despite your efforts, it turns into frustration. Continued frustration is expressed in the form of anger.

This means that there are two levels of work that you have to do in your mind to handle the primary emotions of frustration and fear. This first level of work can be done by applying the three laws, and the second level of work is to actually focus on the task that needs to be done in the world where you exist and operate. It is normal for the mind to go back into the emotion of anger and repeat the whole cycle of anger over and over again.

The cycle of anger begins with the continued frustration that gets triggered with the occurrence of the trigger, which leads to anger, and then, an angry response. Now, this angry response is aimed at stopping the repetition of the undesired thing that leads to frustration.

This angry response is of two kinds—**explosive** or **implosive**. Explosive anger is aimed at attacking the other, whereas implosive anger is attacking the self. Both types intend the stoppage of the undesired thing.

If this is happening to you, you need to know that the mind is giving you a signal that something needs to be done both at the mind level and in the real world as well. If you wish no triggers and expectations ought to disturb you, for this too, the first level of work has to be done in the mind.

CHAPTER
Thirty Three
Dealing with Anger

ANGER CANNOT BE CONTROLLED, BUT FRUSTRATION NEEDS TO BE WORKED ON. People want to control the anger. However, the more you try to control your anger, it is more likely your anger will be of a much higher intensity. Anger cannot be controlled. It is an illusion. The only way out is to deal with anger and work on the source of anger and reduce reasons besides frustration. The first step is to understand that anger that is happening *can* happen. It is possible that what has happened *can* happen. Stop maximising thoughts like, "*I can never imagine this happening to me,*" or "*What has happened is horrible.*"

Stop self-blaming thoughts such as "*How could I have done this?*" These kinds of thoughts will make your mind feel even angrier. It will result in your mind concentrating more and more on the manifestation of anger if you are really swayed by the feelings. The *coming* of the feeling comes is normal but consciously living the feeling is giving strength to the mind. And then, the mind will get conditioned more and more.

At that very moment, remember that you are not the cause and that there is a cause behind the entire occurrence. In fact, there are millions of causes. And it has happened in the past. Your mind is in a set response of mechanism or survival mechanism. Reality is *now*. *Now* is different. An uncontrolled mind wants to behave in accordance with a set perception and response mechanism.

Of course, the expression of anger cannot be called 'good.' But think about what good the event possibly wanted to bring within you. What was missing in you that needed to be corrected? How are you in a better position now, compared to the auto response mechanism of the mind? When you think about this, your mind will rebel stating *"Anger is bad and it is good in no way."* Indeed that is true, but still what was missing in you or what has been created in you to your advantage?

If you find out this answer, you have to assign this as a new label to the manifestation of anger in your mind. So the next time you experience anger, you have to consciously and with effort, find the reason in your mind. Then work on the reason, instead of wasting time in unnecessary self-blame and guilt. When you have done this ten times, your mind will start believing this new label and will not remember the past. Still, the past mechanism will be stored in the memory. However, constant practice will help.

Q: Can we disconnect ourselves from the situation that triggers anger within us?

A: The mind is smart enough to pick up the cues and take you back into the anger-response cycle. So the moment anything connected to the triggers of the anger cycle appears, the mind takes it as a cue.

Taking it out of your sight is taking it out of your mind.

Of course, you can't take everything out of sight. But whatever best you can take away, do it at that very moment. If it is because of someone, tell that person that you are going through a difficulty now and that you need some time for yourself.

- **Walk Away** – Tell the other that you need some time for yourself and you will be back in ten minutes.
- **Cool yourself down** during that time in your own way.
- During that time, **discover the actual trigger point**. Remember it is never because of any person, it is because of something done to you.
- Also, **identify** any **bodily deprivation** of food and water. When you don't have them on time, frustration results in the body and leads to anger.
- Now go back and make an **attempt to repair the situation** (by saying sorry or any gesture). Don't expect the other to welcome you warmly.
- **Don't try to sort out the matter immediately** at that time. **Find the right time** to sort out

the issue, when the other is in the right frame of mind.

- **Create mutually acceptable solutions** for the both of you.

You need to practice this because the anger-response cycle works very fast.

Q: Can we create a new habitual response in place of our anger reaction?

A: Anger cannot be and need not be eliminated; the necessary steps need to be taken. Also, don't think that you will be able to turn everything around right away. It may take some time, but every step will add to your relief. Your genuine steps, commitment, trust in the self and belief in the "supposed to" will bring the change. Work on the root cause, out of which the frustration starts.

Your focus should be this basic cause. The mind makes you feel angry because of certain triggers. Think for a while—*what appears that makes your mind go back to that trap of thinking and feeling cycle?* Understanding the triggers is crucial.

Knowing the trigger will help you find the solution to this pattern. When you are aware of the trigger, see what best you can do towards working on the trigger.

The moment the trigger arrives, know that now that the trigger is there, it is probable that the mind may go back into that cycle. You need to tell to yourself at that moment, "Now when this trigger is there it is normal to feel angry."

Awareness of the pattern and the trigger is a big achievement. Slowly, with a few days of this practice, you will see that the mind has lost the association of the trigger and the feeling. As a result, feelings will cease despite the presence of the trigger.

Q: Is it right to accept our response of anger if it happens despite our effort?

A: Now when you are under the impact of the anger-response cycle, let it happen. The moment you are aware that it is happening to you; your mind will come out of it very quickly and not go very deep in the anger cycle. But you don't have to check whether the mind is coming out or not. Your job is to consider the cycle or response of the mind normal.

Q: How can we replace our image of our anger?

A: This is an active task that needs to be performed at that very moment. The task in this step is to view the trigger as a reminder of the pending work that causes you frustration. As long as you do not do what you are supposed to, the trigger will pull you back to the cycle of anger. So if you view the triggers as a reminder of the undone task, your mind will simply see it as a consequence of the undone task, instead of causing you intense anger—something that happens unconsciously.

The change is possible only if you remember the new statement (or a new view of the old incident) that makes you angry, at that moment. This statement could be anything like—*"Here is my pending work once again."* Start telling your mind the new statement.

The more you practice, this new view of the trigger will become the normal response of your mind. The mind is a very sharp system. The more you train the mind, the more the new layers that form over and over again. Also, your mind will force you to do the needful at the earliest.

A day will come when you will not remember that you used to get angry. It is important to feel happy. Your individual happiness is **INDEPENDENT OF OTHERS**.

You need to start doing all the things that you can to make yourself happy. These can be small little things like eating your favourite dish, watching movies, bicycling, or going to the gym.

PART *Ten*

Shift From Complaints to Meeting The Purpose

CHAPTER

Thirty Four

Knowing the Void

It is true that you are impacted by the feeling of a lack of purpose. Ask yourself a question—"*Why do I feel this purposelessness inside in me?*"

The answer that will emerge is, "*Because I am not able to think about the purpose of my life.*"

Here, it is important to know that in between these two incidents, there is a subtle gap between **thinking about the lack of purpose** and **feeling purposeless** that the mind doesn't understand. Situations exist in the same way for everyone, but you feel purposelessness. Situations are actually passive and happen passively, but the conditioning of your mind makes you feel a sense of purposelessness.

Have you noticed that some people just go on living life without thinking about the purpose, but you feel the purposelessness? People wake up, play their roles during the day, and then come back home by the night and sleep. But you feel the vacuum. So what goes differently for you? You feel a vacuum. This vacuum is experienced only by your mind, and that is what makes it more difficult for you.

Now another question arises, "*Why do you feel the vacuum?*"

Indeed the situation exists in the same way for everyone. The owner of a big business also works in the same monotonous way as a small-time shopkeeper or a housewife who does the same household chores every day. All of them work equally hard. Some do the hard work with their hands, and some with their brains, but the hard work is the same.

Then why do they 'not' feel the vacuum?

Why do you feel the vacuum and why this much?

The answer is—it is the thinking that happens in the subconscious mind that makes it all different for you. Most of the time, people are not aware of their subconscious thoughts. In your case too, maybe you suppress these subconscious thoughts. And whenever they arise, you consciously give yourself logic to suppress them. Finally, these thoughts manifest in form of the purposelessness.

Q: Is it wrong to allow others to decide on our life decisions?

A: This is a common reason why people feel purposelessness in their lives. Most people are not assertive, and due to this, they end up allowing others to drive their life journey. So if you cannot figure out why you are doing what you are doing, it may be because of 'lack of control' over your own life. Maybe you could not plan your career. Or maybe you could not take your life decisions on your own. Maybe you drifted along with the tide of what others said to you. These others could be your own family members or your close ones. This is why, when you see yourself doing what you are doing, you do not see its worth with your own eyes.

It is also possible that you had a plan, but you did not follow through. A few of life's hard knocks may have changed your plan and that may be why you just drifted. The truth is that very few people remain firm about what they decide to do. Like most people, you have never been able to speak for yourself, maybe because you do not trust yourself. As long as you were a child, you looked up to your elders and trusted them with your life decisions. But now, things have changed. Now, you cannot say that you are a kid.

There are very few people who planned out every step and were able to remain untouched by other's interference and indulgence in their lives. This way, they could go 'precisely' where they wanted to go. But because you drifted, it triggered 'the feeling of being lost', and thereby, you have a sense of this purposelessness. You feel clueless about what should be done. This is happening because you have never known that you too can have your say in your own life.

You need to think for yourself and by yourself—*"Should you continue doing what you are doing or should you get out of that place?"* And then, you need to trust the answer and announce it as your decision. For this, it becomes very important to firstly connect to your *Inner Self* and trust that your *Inner Self* has the answer. And when you get your answer, you need to start believing and implementing it.

Q: Why are we so busy that we don't remember our passion?

A: If you are passionate about the main job that you are doing, it is an ideal situation. But for most people, their fight for survival or their *fear* for survival becomes the main reason for dragging the life that they live. They feel purposeless because they are too busy in this 'fight for survival.' The problem comes only to those who think about living their passion. Those who have never known that there is something called passion or purpose have no problem. They live their whole life without awareness, and they keep on doing the same work just like machines.

And there are others like you who are aware that they should live their passion but are too busy merely living a life of survival. In your case, it is obvious that you feel this purposelessness and vacuum because until now, you were too busy with your daily tasks, your job, and other parts of your daily routines. It is like living a bland life, being in the rut.

The first step is to break this thought process in the mind for a while. And only when you do so, you can gain clarity on your purpose. This needs to be done systematically.

Q: Why am I not able to find the purpose of my life?

A: Maybe you want to live a life of purpose, and you are not afraid to make big changes. Your struggle is that for a long time, you have not been able to find your purpose. The first hurdle that exists in your mind is a doubt whether you exist for a purpose. Your mind doubts if there is a meaningful reason for your being or not. Only when you cross this hurdle of disbelief, you will be able to get a few ideas about your purpose. This aspect will be covered in the second part of this course. You will be able to connect the dots and reach your purpose.

Of course, it's hard to defeat the mind and be motivated about the meaningfulness of your life. This is because for a long time you have thought that you have lived a shallow existence, without knowing the purpose. Another truth is that, as of now, you do not know the worth of the life that you have lived till now. However, all of the life that you have lived to this point made a very important contribution to the bigger picture. You will be able to see that 'bigger picture.'

Q: Is it important to get the support of my own people?

A: In your situation, either your close ones have not been there to help you figure out your purpose or they have unknowingly said a few things in past that your mind has perceived negatively. This has probably resulted in a sense of purposelessness in your mind. Those who have a good discussion with the support system find it easy to gain clarity about life.

Q: What Are the Effects of Negative Thinking?

A: This too happens to most people who experience purposelessness. As they say, it is all in the mind. The intensity of the vacuum increases, if you keep thinking about the ideal life day in and day out. Living a purposeful life is important, but merely thinking about the lack of purpose is the biggest source of vacuum. Continued thinking about 'the lack' in life distracts people from their responsibilities and demands of everyday life, whereas one needs to meet these daily responsibilities happily.

Q: Why do we go into self-blame and self-doubt?

A: Your mind irrationally disqualifies the achievements that you have made in the life that you have lived till now. And to top it, your mind blames all the failures on the 'self.' Your mind has a tendency of comparing the Self with other's achievements. It is happening this way maybe because, in the past, someone close has said something negative about you. And it got registered deep in your subconscious awareness. But what has happened cannot be reversed. And it is true that during a tough situation, most people end up blaming the self or others even when they know that this blaming is illogical and damaging.

So ask yourself, "Did your life happen the way it happened only because of you? Or were there other circumstances as well that had their contribution in it?" You probably feel purposelessness because somewhere you have internalised that it all happened because of you and solely you. That is why you are feeling so low about the self at this point when you are actually not. The mind rejects your accomplishments. This is called self- rejection.

However, the truth is that you have done so well, under the given circumstances. This vacuum is there not because life is the way it is, but because you think that the life that you have lived until now was useless when it was actually not. All the parts of the life are like a puzzle. With the life lived till now, you have solved this puzzle quite a bit, and all that you did was needed to solve this puzzle. Every step was needed. At the surface of it, you find the puzzle yet unsolved, but you are very close now.

CHAPTER *Thirty Five*

Sailing Through by Meeting the Purpose

Let us now begin with knowing – "**What is purposefulness?**"

Purposefulness is a useful activity, paid or unpaid, that gives you satisfaction, and interests you most of the time, as a core factor contributing to your happiness.

As you read on, you will be able to discover your purpose. But despite finding the purpose, your mind may not value it.

For this, an important question that needs to be answered is *"Who is this person who has to acknowledge and admire the usefulness and to whom has to it got to be useful to?"* It is very important to know this.

Yes! The first most important person who has to acknowledge the usefulness is **You**.

It is a conscious task to acknowledge the purposefulness of whatever activity you indulge in life-long. Secondly, even if you are not acknowledged by others, you need to acknowledge the fact that your effort is benefitting others directly or indirectly. As a consequence, the energy to put in the effort towards meeting that purpose will come from within you. This effortless effort was also referred as self-actualisation, which means action from within the self, which is not dependent on anything outside.

This **purposefulness then leads to a sense of meaningfulness**. Living meaningfully is about living a life, which has great value or significance. This significance has to be perceived by your *self* first, and then others will acknowledge it as well. Living meaningfully will give you great satisfaction at the end of the day. Only when you meet the purpose, you can experience its meaningfulness.

It is interesting to note that this is a work that needs to be done in the mind first. You have to use your own mind to work on the thought patterns, which will then enable you to live a meaningful life. A new set of thought patterns around the purposefulness needs to be established, deep in the subconscious mind. Your mind may find some difficulty because there are old thought patterns. If you acknowledge the old thought patterns and then, consciously replace them with new thoughts, it will be helpful.

It doesn't matter whether you are an introvert or extrovert. You always have the capability to create a meaningful life. To do this, you need to first allow yourself to explore the purpose, and then, walk in that direction. If you want to live purposefully, you need to engage in the thing that YOU want to do. To do this, you have to commit to always maintain an optimistic perspective, no matter how absurd it gets. It is a conscious task to feel good about life.

To live a meaningful life, you do not have to take yourself from rags to riches or from riches to rags. It is about living a life with 'confidence in self' with the sole agenda of creating happiness. Having a sense of a bigger or a higher purpose is undoubtedly a great source of happiness.

Meaningfulness is not about the actual state of your wealth or achievements, it's more about how you view them. So maybe a decently well-to-do person can be happier than someone who has attained fortunes but lives a life as governed by others, which creates a vacuum inside him or her. The one who lives a purposeful life chooses to craft life on the basis of the purpose that life suggests to him or her. And then, he or she does not measure the level of success on the basis of quantity, but on the level of meaningfulness, which in turn creates quantitative results as well. All you need to see is the progress in meeting the purpose, instead of the quantitative gain.

Q: Can we create a new life now?

A: The mind has a habit of recollecting all the past events. In the process, it misses out on the most important aspect—'the present.' You waste a lot of time thinking about all that has happened. Don't you?

It is funny that what has happened has happened and gone? The good part is that you still have the access to 'the present moment.' 'This present moment' is an opportunity to craft the future. The mind assesses the meaningfulness of life on the basis of the past. It uses this assessment to find out the direction to the future.

The mind is always preoccupied with planning the future. This way, it is busy assessing the past and imagining the future. Yet, there is a very important task which the mind doesn't remember – 'the execution of the plan.' This execution has to be done in the present.

In your situation, your mind has assessed the 'self ' as 'worthless' or inadequate. The mind believes that you will not be able to create any success in the future. But now, you have to put an end to this pattern. To do this, commit to yourself, that you will live the present meaningfully. Only if you live the present meaningfully, only then, in the future, you will be able to say that your life is meaningful.

I repeat – "If you live the present meaningfully, only then, in the future you will be able to say that your life is meaningful." So commit to yourself that you are going to live a meaningful present. In the next few steps, you will learn how to do it. But this commitment to live the present meaningfully is the first step.

Q: How do I find the purpose of my existence?

A: If you look at all the living or non-living objects around, you will realise that everything exists in this world for fulfilling some purpose. Everything is caused. Everything is created for some purpose. Now, look at your hands. Nature has created this body in this world, to fulfill some purpose. You need to forcefully make your mind believe that you too have been created for some unique purpose. This will help you in taking the next few steps.

Q: How to know what I am good at?

A: After believing that you too exist for some core purpose, this is an active task that you need to do. Take a sheet of paper and randomly list down the things that you like doing. These may be things that you appreciate about yourself or something that others appreciate you for. But they can also be things that you have never shared with others or something that you never did. When you start writing, your mind may rebel and deny that there is nothing that you like doing. But this is a conscious task to do.

List down all random things. It can be reading, writing, eating, anything. It is important to first believe that you are good and you have these areas of interest. It doesn't matter whether you are good in these areas or not, or whether you do them casually. These are like areas of interest or things that you do freely and comfortably without thinking that they are tasks. Tell your mind that at least ten such things exist. Keep writing. And after when you are done, read all of the things for a few moments. And then identify the top three areas out of the list. This is very simple. For this, you need to just follow your gut feeling and tick the best, the second best and the third best.

After you have ticked the top three areas, you need to consciously believe that you can create huge success in these areas even in terms of money or position as well. Do you know any of these areas can be turned really big in terms of money and appreciation in the world?

Remember the **primary goal** is not money; it is **satisfaction and meaningfulness**. Of course, the **secondary goal** has to be **money** because money is a resource to make this purpose big enough. When money becomes the primary objective, the passion goes away. **The third motivator** is **constant growth** in terms of position and impact that can be created if you follow your passion. And because these areas are things that you like doing, your mind would want to discover more about them. You need to be the best and create something new in this area. This spirit is needed to be continually motivated.

Q: What is the purpose of my life?

A: Out of the top three areas that you have selected from the list, you need to find out the one that you feel the most passionate about. For a moment just believe that your *Inner Self* is aware of your passion. While concentrating on the *Inner Self*, all the other thoughts need to be stopped. Have faith that your *Inner Self* will reveal that top one purpose to you. It may be a hazy abstract hint that your *Inner Self* will bring up to your conscious awareness. Just trust that hint. It can be anything. It can be anything out of the three that you see yourself comfortably living for.

Everything has a scope of becoming meaningful, and everything can grow big. Even if your *Inner Self* has revealed some voluntary service as your passion, it definitely has a scope of becoming big. This can happen only when you see meaningfulness in it. Of course, you have to actively make it big. A lot of stress is placed on making it big. This is done because the mind has a habit of comparing the achievements of the self with that of others.'

If your passion grows big, your mind will get the needed motivation. The mind loves to play the game that gives a thrill. Only the things that can grow big will appeal to the mind. The mind, like a baby, will get bored if there are no new challenges in the game. The area that you have ticked may appear funny or weird to you. Your mind may also think that others may find your choice funny or weird. Your mind will throw around a lot of doubt. This is normal. But remember that it is your passion.

You will be able to make it big in this area, only when 'you' are convinced. And a day will come when you reach success. It is funny that everyone will praise you for the same idea the day you reach success and not today. So the success is your **choosing** this idea as your passion today. But the question arises—*"Who can convince you that this is your passion?"* It is **you**. So convince your own self that it is your *Inner Self* that has revealed this area as your passion. You do not have to doubt it. If you do, after a few years, you will repent again. So do not compare this new journey on the basis of the time that it will take. Also, do not compare your success with that of others.

If you look up to someone who has already attained success in the area that you have chosen, see that he or she has also put so much effort and belief in that area to make it big. This is your journey. And your journey cannot be compared to any other person's journey. Everybody has appeared in this world for a specific journey. And everyone has to complete the journey, and only then, he or she can go. So trust your journey and accept that your journey is unique and has its own gestation period. There is no question of how much time it will take, because when it is about an experience and not the time, only then there are accomplishments.

Also, if you find any difficulty in arriving at that purpose, tell your mind that it will occur to you in some time. You need to keep yourself open and then suddenly, you will get the hint about your purpose.

Q: How do I become focused?

A: Even if it is a hazy idea, it will get more refined and crystalised with time. You need to actively craft it with commitment. It is important to have a strong belief and be committed to actions aimed at this purpose of your life. Only commitment towards the purpose will give you the satisfaction that you always longed for. You need to take baby steps towards meeting your purpose. Walking step-by-step, a day will come when you start loving everything about your purpose. It's your vision that will make it meaningful for you, and then, the world will also start believing in you.

The world will acknowledge it only when you have no need for its acknowledgement. It should give you happiness. When you work effortlessly with joy, your effort will create success in terms of money and acknowledgement. This area will give you enough challenge and growth opportunity, only if you are committed. This way, you will be able to create your own unique offering to the world, by meeting your purpose every day. You have been in the vacuum for such a long time, so it is normal if the negative thoughts of the past impact you.

Let them happen whenever they come. It is normal. It is important to not have to have an expectation that the mind will always think positive. So when you experience negative thoughts like fear, self-doubt, doubt about whether you are doing the right thing, just be aware that it is happening and allow it to happen. The moment you are aware that it is happening to you, your mind will come out of it very quickly. You do not have to check whether the mind is coming out or not. Your job is to accept the cycle of negative thoughts as 'normal.' Allow the mind to complete the cycle of negative thinking.

Q: How can I become successful in life?

A: When you take your every step towards living the purpose, you will get an amazing sense of satisfaction. You need to bring the best out of you in this direction and create small wins. If you have people in your support system, you need to request them to respect and motivate you towards your purpose. Share your small wins with them.

Remember it is about the journey and not the destination. The journey should give you meaning with every milestone that you arrive at. Thereafter, be open to receiving pleasant surprises in the form of small success that you get every day.

Conclusion

The initial parts of the book helped you gain a good understanding of the Truth Behind Divine Play, i.e., the *Larger Self*. And the later part included practical ways of handling life issues.

Have you heard of the word *'Leela'*? *The Leela. "Leela"* is a word derived from Sanskrit which in English means "play." *Leela* is a way of describing the interplay of so many *"I's"* and forms the *"Larger I."* The *"I"* or "Self " in you and the *"I"* of a few your friends combines and forms the manifestation of the *"Larger I"* in the form of a picnic. It is the macrocosmic actions of the manifestation of the *"Larger I."*

In some scriptures and schools, it is also refered to as *Maya*. "Maya" is a Sanskrit word which in English means "illusion" and "magic." The word "Maya" has a connotation of a "magic show", an illusion where things appear to be present but are not what they seem."

The manifestation of the "*Larger I*" is referred to as "Maya" or illusion because this manifestation exists, but is constantly changing and thus is spiritually or even scientifically unreal. The power or the principle or the "*Larger I*" that conceals its true creator is always hidden.

Even Science has discovered that the matter is always changing. The atoms are changing at an unimaginable speed which cannot be measured. The chemical and physical composition of all matter is constantly undergoing change. This is why things and this world appear to be real, like the light of the bulb that appears to be constant and so-called real, when it is actually not. But indeed, for all practical purposes, you have no other choice but to call it real. Of course, at an atomic level, the reality at a particular point is not the same reality after one second.

If you look at the building around you, or even the mountain, or your closed ones and your life, it is constantly changing. It is not how it was ten years ago or how it was a year ago or a week ago. If you see very carefully, all this is also not the same as it was yesterday. There is movement. Ask yourself—"Who is doing it?" The answer is that the interplay of so many millions, billions, and uncountable *"Larger I's"* in the form of *"I"* are doing it.

All this interplay can be realised by personally experiencing the truth and *Inner Self Integration* facilitates this realisation. With all the learning that you have had, you can now understand the existence of the *'Leela'* and you can play your part of the *'Leela'* fairly well. Now, you are aware of what is happening outside, i.e., '*The Leela*' and 'What you need to do from the '*I*' as the character of the movie, in response to the '*Leela*.'

This book was an attempt to help you connect to the Self within you and teach you simple ways of living life to the fullest.

Live Happy, Live Fully, Life is Beautiful...

Made in the USA
Middletown, DE
02 January 2020

82412214R00246